Dedication

To my children, Mark and Britta,
to whom I've always been very close,
and to Linda's children, Scott, Jody and Kara,
to whom I know she would have remained close as well.

Chapter One
Ideal Tournament, Ideal Job

On a sticky, hot August afternoon, spectators stream away from Firestone Country Club's Irish green fairways knowing for certain they've witnessed golf history.

Jack Nicklaus just won the 57th PGA Championship.

Anything but ho-hum, even though it's the Golden Bear's fourth PGA crown.

This Sunday, Nicklaus displays his legendary cool. He comes up with a 71 score to win. His sun-bleached bangs sweaty and mussed, Nicklaus leaves Firestone after posing with a three-gallon-sized, curved handle PGA trophy, taking his $45,000 in winnings with him.

But it's Saturday's third round that's causing the buzz among the exiting crowd. Nicklaus performs what some call "wizardry." And people are reliving the magnificent 67 he shot. Oh, the magic of his 16th-hole performance.

What Nicklaus does to whip up the crowd on Saturday is take on the "monster," nicknamed as Firestone's signature challenge hole for its dogleg shape and downhill slope. He realizes when he's standing at the 16th tee, he should have in hand a three-wood instead of his driver. Nicklaus admits, "I guess I must have started to be too pleased with myself, because now I got downright sloppy."

Near boiling in Akron's steaming heat, he makes an uncharacteristic decision to not retrieve what he wants from caddie Greek-born Angelo Argea. (This gray curly-haired chap is uniquely a celebrity in his own right.)

Then Nicklaus hits with the driver. He ends up in a hazard. His third shot is in the rough surrounded by trees. So next, he lofts a 9-iron shot over a 30-foot tree onto the green. And then he sinks a 30-foot par putt.

This mastery, coupled with Sunday's precise play, gives him a two-shot advantage over Australian Bruce Crampton.

To this day, Nicklaus relishes this 57th PGA win in a long life of wins. He describes the play in his autobiography, "My Story."

"The ball cleared the top of the tree by about three inches, and the lake by a couple of paces, and stopped thirty feet beyond the pin. And now, of course, it would be just too anticlimactic not to make the putt."

The Akron, Ohio gallery is thrilled to see such a display of brilliance, relayed to a large TV audience at home.

During Sunday's final hoopla, I'm busy packing in an off-white trailer placed to the side of the south golf course. It has been a long, long year. My August-to-August job at the PGA tournament office helping to set up this much-esteemed tournament in my hometown is almost over.

I can't help thinking as I watch crowds flow to the parking lots back in 1975 that most know nothing about the murder and mayhem playing out earlier behind the scenes.

This horrible thing in my past is something you'd think I'd live with in some faraway sense. Yet every single time that my memories float back to that time, one of my sharpest feelings is surprise at what a fresh power my life back then still has over me.

Sure enough, decades have passed swiftly. I go from daring youth to spirited middle age to senior gad-about. It's time on the 35th anniversary of the 57th PGA Championship to write an account of the whole story. And to explain the circumstances which led to my being connected with such a tragic mishmash of events.

I know this will be one of the most difficult tasks I have attempted. It will be sad when detailing this tragedy as I knew it to unravel. It will also be puzzling and embarrassing for me to face truths about myself as a young woman. But I hold no reservations at this point.

The beginning of this story must establish Firestone Country Club. From an almost folksy beginning, the club – set in rolling hills gently bringing the visitor from a once-smoky city to raindrop clear countryside – has a history like no other in the United States. Harvey Firestone commissioned the club for his rubber company employees and others. You can almost see his wide grin as he swings to open Firestone Country Club in 1929.

Many upgrades later, Firestone has a stellar past of hosting more major tournaments than any other course. In 2009, the club celebrates 80 years with 55 years straight providing tournament golf. No other club has this sterling tradition.

When you grow up in Akron, you are physically and emotionally touched by this course and the surrounding serene area. You feel a special connection whether watching a tournament live from Akron on TV, buying a gallery ticket for an event or even walking and playing at Firestone Metropolitan Park across the way.

Yet, fully aware of what a rare opportunity it is to be part of the prestige of Firestone Country Club, I must confess right off that I don't really want this PGA job.

I prefer to stay home with my kids, ages one and six. I quit my newspaper job I held from 1969 to 1972 at the *Akron Beacon Journal*. My husband Larry and I are doing okay on his paycheck as business editor at the *Beacon Journal* largely covering the omnipresent tire industry and my free-lancing, including some writing for the newspaper.

But then, we buy a four-bedroom house near the treed campus of Kent State University where I went to school. I am quite fond of having the children in their own rooms finally after a cramped two bedroom duplex, also in Kent.

Like all young couples in their first home, we need money when the PGA offer comes along. This is a one-year commitment as an office assistant that pays $200 a week plus a hinted-at bonus. It's an ideal set up because it isn't a demanding, long-term deal. But still, I stew in my own juices for a bit over working full time.

Finally, saying, "I adore you, oh my babies, but Mama has to go to work," I hand over my children to babysitters. Did I mention I didn't golf back then?

I meet Linda McLain, a fellow PGA staffer, at a time when our lives are hectic blurs of getting sleepy-headed kids ready in the morning so we can be ship-shape for the job.

The PGA task is shorn of its glamour early on. I wish for something grassy in terms of our satellite Firestone Country Club office locale. Championship golf to me means hills and valleys, sand traps and bird-filled ponds.

But instead the PGA headquarters is set up in downtown Akron where two block-length department stores, Polsky's and O'Neil's, and a handful of restaurants and small retail outlets stretch for about two non-character miles.

PGA urban style is in Cascade Plaza – one of the few high rises – on one of the top floors. Not even a storefront for golfers such as Lee Trevino or Johnny Miller to pop in and chat. But then downtown is about seven miles from the golf course.

These offices are rent-free for the PGA. Linda and I hole up in what is storage space for the large law office of Roetzel & Andress. Out of these tiny rooms, there are magnificent views of downtown, which historically is centered at a staircase of locks near the Ohio and Erie canals. Akron means "summit" in Greek, thus the Summit County where it's located.

I'm supposed to handle public relations as well as work with the volunteers. Linda toils as the receptionist/typist. The work itself proves most menial. Accustomed to a newsroom where there is incessant shoptalk, backbiting and deadline tension, I'm not so used to being so bored in a job. The enormous egos and glib remarks make newspapering an interesting career.

For the PGA, the only "writing" I end up doing is creating blurbs for the daily program when the tournament is in full swing, Aug. 4-10, 1975.

Linda and I pass the time in the small office, space donated by lawyer Richard Guster who's (volunteer) general chairman of the 57th PGA Championship, by talking about everything, from what's on TV the night before to our kids' latest follies.

This is a new kind of relationship for me. Co-workers in the past are friendly but not near this cozy. But with Linda, it's like being locked in a small room for hours and hours with only one magazine. You read the thing from cover-to-cover. We became close-knit and supportive of each other.

Chapter Two
Settling into the PGA Office

At first, Linda seems content enough with her daily life. Her appearance isn't always neat but neither is mine. I have the haggard characteristics of a working mom – runs in my pantyhose and scuffed up shoes. One day, I show up for work with Oreo cookie stains on my flare leg tan slacks. Neither of us has career clothes and we look like the clean up crew next to the polished attorneys coming and going from our floor.

We also lack beauty shop hairdos, those sleek helmet styles pelted to the head with Aqua Net. We dab our make-up on when we get to work and comment how nice it is to drink coffee in peace without children tugging at us.

With three children, ages 2, 6 and 7, and a husband who works in the factory at Firestone Rubber Co., 27-year-old Linda struggles with finances on a more frantic level than I do. Yet she has the self-assurance of someone who once knew a more cushy life.

I should note we both got our PGA jobs because we know someone. I have done some sports stories for the *Beacon Journal* and came to know Firestone public relations man Dale Antram, front and center with the 57th PGA organizing. As a reporter, I covered ladies golf tournaments (LPGA) at the St. Lucie, Fla., Hilton Inn Country Club and the U.S. Women's Open at the Kahkwa Country Club in Erie, Pa., both in 1971.

My getting the 57th PGA job is helped, I'm sure, by the fact that my husband is business editor. Linda's uncle, James Miller and married to the sister of Linda's mother, is a big shot at General Tire, back in the day when the tire factories dominate in our sooty corner of the world.

Linda has faith in herself at work. She makes her office telephone calls and does her typing with snappy confidence. Well-spoken, she is an attractive redhead with crystal blue eyes and creamy fair skin. Her best trait has to be her voice – it's melodic; I guess it could be called sexy. Anyway she comes across as very likeable on the phone.

Her weight – 145 pounds – bothers her. But at 5 feet 5 inches, she's far from chunky. I have the impression that despite the job pressures, kids and housework, she likes earning money, getting dressed for work and talking with people.

Linda is quite interested in how my husband and I manage our household budget. She asks me to look at her bills and her plans to pay them. I give it a shot but I'm a somewhat ditzy 28-year-old who married in college. So I went from my father to a husband. I do know how to spend money on eclectic clothes though. My husband, older and much, much wiser at age 35, handles our finances. Still, after my "wisdom" is passed along to Linda, she opens a savings account.

What in the world do we do in this PGA job? With the help of someone very capable, Margaret Garforth, a woman in her mid-50s who's in the next office as a blazingly efficient secretary for the tournament director, we drum up business and goodwill for the 57th Championship.

Initially, we contact country clubs in Ohio and surrounding states to request their mailing lists. Then we type up envelopes to mail out brochures listing the ticket packages. ASAP we need to start selling PGA tickets, with a big push coming up for the holiday season.

"Hello, I'm calling from the PGA Championship," begins the sales pitch. You would think this would open doors wide. But most people respond for us to mail out a brochure; not many pony up for tickets in these early months.

I pretend to run the place when the couple hired to get this golf tournament going are out of town. Our boss is J. Edwin Carter who's busy wrapping up the previous PGA Championship held in Hawaii and lobbying to get the 58th PGA Championship in Washington, D.C. So he's in and out of the office a lot in 1974 and 1975, greeting us initially with the caustic remark," I don't know why they are paying you so much!"

His wife, M.J. Carter, still tanned from Hawaii, handles her blustery husband and does the important work of the office such as cordially meeting VIPs in Akron. We joke a lot with her about the culture shock of coming from breezy easy Hawaii to our little tire-making "paradise" of belching factories and blue-collar standards.

"You look so young," says M.J. to me early on in our meeting. I do. I have fringy bangs and long chestnut brown hair. I wear the same make-up from college – black eyeliner, pale lips and heavy foundation, all cleansed off at night with a smear of Noxzema brand cream because I like the menthol smell. I'm super skinny, less than 110 pounds at 5'5 and have bony chicken wing arms.

As for my PGA ascent, Ed Carter is right about one thing. I'm a highly paid go-fer. The average rubber worker union contract at that time is $5.50 an hour. So I should feel guilty that I'm just sitting on my behind earning almost as much as a sweaty, hard-working factory worker. But I did lack those great benefits – no vacation, holiday pay, etc.

Anyway, I fetch Carter's lunch on days he's in town.

"Two hotdogs with mustard." Yes, sir. Cost: 90 cents. He gives me a dollar and I return from the next door building coffee shop with his wieners and 10 cents change, which he always keeps. No tip.

Ed Carter is a strange bird. To us, he's a bitter taste of medicine. We love when he isn't in the office. He grumbles constantly about the shortcomings found in Akron. Hey, I spent my whole life here. The theme song I used to carry around in my head is 1965's the Animal's "We Gotta Get Out of This Place." It goes: "In this dirty old part of the city where the sun refused to shine."

Still, it's one thing for a native to want to flee the place for lack of fresh opportunity and quite another for a newcomer swooping into town to trash talk Acorn (my pet name for Rubber City). Despite the grimy, gray winters, this is not a forlorn place to live. I find more than a sufficient amount of mischief growing up; Akron is not even a bore as I grew older.

In Akron, there is not only a vital history to nourish one's need to belong but future prep work is available galore.

Carter is sweet and gracious when anyone from the PGA is in the office, especially Guster and the other higher up volunteers. Then the minute they leave, he goes into a rant about how they are failing to raise the big bucks necessary to run this tournament.

In his late 60s, he has a shiny face and cobweb eyebrows with a receding hairline. When he smiles his false grin, he looks somewhat kindly. But his round face grows greasy-like when he mutters angry words.

M.J., who puffs away on a cigarette during her husband's tirades, reassures him it will all come together. It always does. And Firestone C.C. is hardly breaking the seal here on hosting the top shelf PGA Championship. In 1974-75, this is the course's third time in 15 years.

The only gripe I hear from M.J., much younger than the bear she's married to, is finding satisfaction with a local hairdresser. "No one can do it right," she moans. She wears the stiff-as-a-board hairstyle so popular.

Their job also entails selling advertisements for a cumbersome book that will be sold to PGA golf tournament attendees. It's magazine style, with some copy but mostly advertising.

This book is a PGA tradition with Carter's stamp all over it. In a *Sports Illustrated* story dated December 1961, the magazine talks about Carter "sandbagging" loyal club members to put advertising in this hefty book. (What kind of money are we talking about here? The 1961 PGA book made a $50,000 profit with Carter back then getting a cut, making his salary $100,000 a year in 1961, notes *SI*.)

The opening of our 266-page book is a page from President Gerald Ford. And speaking of this president, by 1975 the country is in a recession with 9.2 percent unemployment. Companies such as Foot-Joy and Acushnet Golf Equipment are a given for buying ad space but the locals are dragging a little on signing the contracts.

But then, Akron is at the beginning of the rubber industry's eventual exodus from town to factories in the Deep South. Factories that are rolling out tires now are seeing the tail end of the successful years. Years that someone like my grandfather, a Romanian immigrant who spoke broken English, could make a healthy living in a manufacturing job. Buildings three to five stories high with brick walls and ornate clock towers where workers once handmade tires are still everywhere in Akron but the action is slowing down.

Ironically, one of the advertisements that comes in for the PGA book is from Yeargin Construction Inc., located in Greenville, S.C.. The company has just completed a 35-acre Firestone factory in Wilson, N.C. Steel-belted radial passenger tires are on the roll, miles south of Akron, off a complex, mechanical assembly line.

If ever there is an ominous financial cloud on the horizon, it's the implication from this advertisement.

Chapter Three
Laid Off Tragedy

At the PGA office, while I work with the core of volunteers, the staff is never part of any planning breakfasts and lunches. Still, on a regular basis, I am face-to-face with one of those volunteers such as Taffy Fair, chairman, clubhouse credentials, or Kit Cassidy, scoring.

Golf tournaments conjure up decorum and good manners. That I expect. But it's also weird after being so connected to the hubbub of a newsroom in the past where gallows humor and cuss words ruled. Social upheaval surrounding the shootings at Kent State University happened about 20 miles away five years earlier. The Vietnam War also ends in 1975 as Communist forces take Saigon and South Vietnam surrenders. So, in a way, it's reassuring to know that Firestone traditions remain intact. Yet it is a strange intersection for me to be witnessing.

I have had previous exposure to the country club set. While at the *Beacon Journal,* I cover some fashion stories and remember a rather sad afternoon when I drank too much bubbling Cold Duck at the elegant Portage Country Club. I was covering a Bar Association Auxiliary luncheon. Or rather I was sipping along with the lawyers' wives. My husband, Larry, has to cart me home so I can sober up with a cold shower before writing my story.

"You are not supposed to drink with them," he scolded. "You are supposed to be reporting on them." It was my first exposure to ladies who drink at noon.

Anyway, with this great background of covering Akron fashion, I can't imagine why the PGA ladies want me to order their tournament uniforms of sleeveless, navy blue Izod dresses with white stitching. Wearing polyester knit in the full height of steaming summer made little sense. But the joke is on me – I am ordered to order one of these dresses for myself.

I am in the vortex of country club protocol. And tradition – let's not forget that. Out of the eight members of the 57th PGA Championship Executive Committee, seven are white males. The lone woman is listed as Mrs. Bruce W. Rogers Jr. But I should talk. At the time, I held a Polsky's department store credit card (I still have it as a lark). It is in the name of Mrs. Larry N. Froelich.

I am earning money independently though. My daughter Britta's lime green shag carpet in her pink canopy bedroom is safe for the time being. And my son, Mark, can continue his education at the Kent State University School where we pay tuition.

Linda likes the money too. She makes a dentist appointment and for the first time in years she has her teeth cared for. I can still picture her rubbing her finger over her back molars after some drilling dentist episode.

Her aunt, James Miller's wife, Eva, gives her a pair of high heel shoes. She keeps these in her desk drawer and wears them only at work. At Christmastime, I give Linda a bag of sugar to make cookies as sugar is priced sky-high.

In all our daily comings and goings, it is obvious Linda has a huge crush on her husband, Tom. She doodles "Tom & Linda" on every note pad she touches while making her phone calls for those mailing lists.

Margaret and I make fun of this practice. We love our husbands, we agree, but the sun doesn't rise and set; know what I mean? We keep these catty comments to ourselves though because Linda is happy to be stuck in this "going steady" phase.

Then Tom is laid off at Firestone the Friday before Christmas and Linda's warm glow and hustle change.

I don't find this unusual. Labor strife and job uncertainty are nothing new living in this one-industry town. Akron's powerful United Rubber Workers (URW) union, formed in 1935, has a high number of 190,500 members in 1974. There are constant strikes and layoffs involving the Big Four – Goodyear, Goodrich, General and Firestone. Workers collect money from strike funds and unemployment compensation. Still, the psychological factor is always critical to consider when a person loses a job.

There is a collective spirit of support in the community with all this union vs. Big Four strife. But that doesn't help much at home when you are eating bologna sandwiches daily and the wife is wringing her hands in the background.

Linda's work gradually becomes so poor that I view her as worthless in the office. I do both our work but don't tell boss Carter or his wife. Linda's smiling eyes change to those of a frightened person. She is consumed with Tom's unemployment.

I know that her lack of sleep is due to Tom's keeping her up all night because he is so distressed about being laid-off at Firestone. She tells me this. So what can I do? Squeal on her to the PGA folks?

After the holidays, she confides that Tom had a nervous breakdown when they were first married because of the stress and responsibility. This is entirely new information.

In early February, Linda attempts to tell me what a nightmare her life is. She doesn't mention physical abuse but she says how mean he is to her. "Please don't tell anybody," she pleads," because this office is so connected with Firestone."

My first reaction is, "Why are you married to someone like this?"

She answers without hesitation, "I love Tommy and I want to be married to him."

I suggest she get professional help. She does. They go to a marriage counselor the next week. But then Linda is upset because this session is only to fill out forms, pay their money and set up future appointments.

On a bitterly cold February day, Tom takes her out to a burger joint for lunch.

She comes back in less than an hour, very distressed. She's profusely sweating, her cheeks flushed and splotchy. She immediately picks up the phone and calls the marriage counselor. When she hangs up, she tells me she really feels Tom needs to be in a hospital but that the counselor tells her to try a new approach.

When Tom begins his verbal harassment, she's to say, "Tom, we've discussed all this and I just don't want to talk about it anymore."

I am astounded at this advice. Maybe I am weary of this distracting soap opera playing out while we are trying to get into the lively spirit of this upcoming golf spectacular. I set her up with some advice. I tell her being passive isn't the answer. "You need to speak up," I implore her.

This is my personality – to be outspoken and impulsive as my husband can attest.

That night, Tom stabs Linda 13 times with a 10-inch blade butcher knife.

Chapter Four
Coming Back Home

To know the rest of this story, it is necessary to jump ahead to 1989. I know this seems strange but trust me, I have packed everything I know into retelling this. It took me a number of years to be in a place where I realized Linda's murder was something I ought to look into. And even more years to appreciate the layers of a nurturing environment Akron always provided me.

So flash ahead to 1989. I guess I always thought I'd be called some day to testify at Tom's trial. I had seen him a few times when he stopped by our PGA office – before and after he lost his job. I couldn't for anything see where this exciting, handsome guy Linda had led me to believe she was married to is in Tom. He has a certain cocky swagger – but this is before he's laid-off. He has droopy brown eyes, thinning brown hair and a scraggly moustache, and is a lean and muscled 5 feet 8 inches. After the job loss, he seemed to have withdrawn in a shell, not making eye contact when he came in to see Linda.

I had given a deposition to an assistant county prosecutor in 1975. But then I waited and nothing happened as my own personal life went bonkers. By 1989 though, I was fairly settled as a 42 year old. After a divorce from Larry, joint custody of my children with my son Mark moving to Detroit so my ex-husband could work at the *Detroit Free Press*, a quick remarriage and divorce to a Goodyear worker, a move to Florida and a budding relationship with photographer Ray Bassett (whom I finally married in 1995 after many, many ups and downs), I was about at peace as an unconventional woman could be.

The amazing thing is I had gotten my newspaper career back at the excellent *St. Petersburg Times*. I was hired in early 1983. So by 1989, I am established there, first as the food writer and then as the higher profile TV critic. I am covering events such as Oprah's Chicago one-year anniversary of her talk show – splashy stories that gained attention. So I was no longer this lost Akron girl looking for something.

I survive the '70s but obviously with remorse.

What prompts me to find out about Linda is the horrifying Joel Steinberg trial in all the newspapers. I am upset by the boxer-like bashed face of survivor Hedda Nussbaum and the beating death of her daughter Lisa.

I begin to feel strongly after reading about all these people noticing abuse and not doing anything about it. I need to get myself back to Akron and find out everything I can about Linda's death and the aftermath.

I actually ask the *St. Petersburg Times* if I can do a story on domestic violence. At the time, before online news put newspapers in the toilet, this newspaper always says "yes" to such an adventure, no matter where it is. My job gives me the time off; I pay for the airline ticket and other expenses.

I clear up my schedule, my parents come from Sebring to take care of my 15-year-old daughter, Britta, and by February 1989, I fly to Akron. Realities of those freezing winters I left behind seven years earlier to move to Florida all come back. Chapped lips, cold toilet seats, dry static furnace heat, pot holes the size of a child's swimming pool. These are nasty experiences all around.

I land at Akron/Canton airport on February 5 without a winter coat, boots or scarf. It's nine degrees out. So much for my sister's pre-trip words: "We're having a mild winter. Temperatures are in the 50s. We'll grill chicken out."

Oh well, this will also give me a visit with my 20-year-old son at Kent State. And I can at long last, look into the circumstances of Linda's murder.

I can't remember Linda's last name or the exact date of her death. But fortunately, my former newspaper, the *Beacon Journal,* has an ace librarian in Cathy Tierney. I visit her at the newspaper right away.

Within 10 minutes, Tierney finds, "Mother of 3 Stabbed to Death in Home" on microfilm dated Feb. 5, 1975. In part, the story states Linda McLain was "found dead on arrival at City Hospital where her husband, Herbert (real name), 33, was fair with what police said was an apparent overdose of pills that he normally took for high blood pressure."

The article continues that police found a suicide note. Detectives believe this is written by Tom, a laid-off Firestone pipe fitter. Police won't release the contents of the note.

The story states Tom would be charged with murder when released from the hospital.

The microfilm copy of Linda's obituary, dated Feb. 7, 1975, has a thumbprint-size photo. This looks like a high school graduation kind because her eyes are full of promise.

The clip file has more. A story dated Oct. 17, 1975 carries this headline: "Hospital, prison for wife-killer."

It explains that while the county judge finds Tom "legally competent in that he understood the nature of the charge and could help in his defense," he is also "mentally ill in that he does not have the capacity to use self-control in his activities."

Tom is committed to Massillon State Hospital for the Criminally Insane. When he recovers, he is to serve seven to 25 years in prison for voluntary manslaughter.

Tom pleaded and had been sentenced. So that's why I didn't hear more.

But there is more on Tom – a surprise for sure. As I'm rolling through the microfilm, Tierney shouts, "He's dead." I have goose bumps. I figure Tom is 47 years old by now and out on his insanity plea.

But no. "Herbert D. (Tom) McLain, 38, died peacefully in his sleep Saturday, May 17, (1980)."

The obit concludes, "Mr. McLain is survived by his beloved children," then ages 13, 12 and 7.

There is a smiling, also very young, photo of Tom and a tiny American flag as an extra decoration on the notice to mark that he served honorably in the Air Force.

Boy, am I confused. Does this mean he is out of the mental institution in five years after killing Linda? His obit has an address where he lives in Akron. Does this mean he is living there with his children? How did he die? Yes, high blood pressure but age 38 is pretty young to pass away.

I take a break from this research and call the prosecutor's office. The only thing I was able to do before I left Florida was to establish that I am a newspaper reporter and would need to look at a murder file. Without the McLain last name or date of the crime, I can only establish this introduction. After quickly relating my new-found material with the receptionist there, she says to stop by later that afternoon and the file will be available.

Back to my newspaper research, my memory is refreshed on a point I long forgot. Two prominent Akron families are involved in this little-publicized case of a PGA staffer murdered by her husband. Linda and Tom seem threadbare poor. I never hear any mention of family helping out such as a treat of a dinner and movie out.

Tom's stepfather is Dominic Sanginiti, whose family owns a famous, fairly pricey Italian restaurant in downtown Akron. And Linda's uncle (her mother's sister's husband) is (or was) president of the tire group at General Tire. It is James Miller who got her the PGA job.

At the prosecutor's office, the file is not to be had. It is explained to me that a file this old is kept in another building, across the street, and will be retrieved first thing the next morning. The weather is freezing outside so I can understand why a file isn't immediately made available to a Florida interloper.

So I go to my sister's for the night, take my son Mark and his Kent State roommates to dinner and sit totally pre-occupied with all these unanswered questions.

I wake up three times that night, tossing and turning under my flannel sheets.

Chapter Five
More Digging for the Facts

Morning finally arrives. At the prosecutor's office, I'm handed two thick folders. But before I can dive in, I am told an assistant prosecutor wants to talk with me. This is the last thing a reporter wants to hear.

Fred Zuch is not in his office at the time but his secretary Becky calls him and hands me the phone. All he wants to tell me is that there is a lot of confidential psychiatric information in the files.

"I probably shouldn't let you see this," says Zuch. "But since McLain is dead, what the heck." He tells me to use my own discretion in what I chose to use in my story.

This sounds reasonable so I find a seat in the large library and open the first file. I'm not emotionally girded for the first thing I see. There are maybe half a dozen photographs from Linda's autopsy. She looks cold dead bluish with slashes all over that creamy skin. I slam the file shut and take a few minutes to compose myself.

When I reopen the file, I push the photographs to the back and begin reading.

I find the suicide note. This note was found on top of the refrigerator in the kitchen, according to the police report. It isn't addressed to anyone, nor is it signed.

Tom has horrible spelling, so I've corrected that aspect of the note: "Just before I met Linda, I thought my life was at a dead end. I met this girl at the Pogo Restaurant. I asked her out. The guy I doubled with dated her girlfriend Linda. She was very pretty and seemed a little headstrong.

"I was in a depressed mood at the time. My dad died. My grandfather died. And I got into a car accident and lost my driver's license. I was very lonely and depressed. I was working at Goodyear at the time, building tires which I hated because I wanted back into the trade.

"I lived in a one room apartment in Ellet. I kept everything inside me, the hurt, the loneliness. I was dating another girl at the time. I was going with her and didn't feel like seeing (anyone) except Shirley. I loved her very much but my personal problems interfered with her, so she left. I didn't blame her. And now I'm at that point again. I love my wife. I see what I did wrong and I can't stand the pain. I feel it's too late as usual. I tried. I love you."

In the file, psychiatrists and psychologists have different opinions about what is wrong with Tom. After the homicide, he is tense and hysterical. He cries during much of his mental health interviews. He isn't hallucinating but he's considered dangerous by those examining him.

His body shakes, he runs his hands through his hair constantly and "he has great difficulty in articulating his words."

The personal data – parents divorced when he was five, his father was a heavy drinker, raised by mother and grandparents, played first string basketball in high school, went to trade school to be a plumber and steam pipe fitter, married nine years, smokes two packs of cigarettes a day, golfed with a two handicap, and drinks "a couple of beers now and then."

Tom has a long history of psychiatric hospitalizations and treatments, dating back to 1967, when he sought treatment in a Kansas City mental hospital for his nerves. One report notes that Tom became anxious and withdrawn at the age of 10 when a school friend drowned.

Tom has no police record, but there is evidence from both the police report and Linda's autopsy that he abused his wife.

The Feb. 5, 1975 police report states: "There were many bruises on her breasts, arms, face and ears. Some of the bruises were old, being shades of yellow and brown. Others were fresh being dark red." The coroner finds brown and yellow bruises on her breasts and thighs. Tom is a wife beater? I wonder if violence went on all of their married life?

On the night of the murder, Tom and Linda had dinner, put the kids to bed and make love. Tom is unhappy.

"She acted like she didn't care," Tom told police. "My mind went bananas. I grabbed something and I hurt her. I thought she was killing me, killing me with words."

More details are in other reports. After they had made love, Tom came out in the living room and sat on the sofa. Linda followed him. She was dressed in a short nightgown.

They exchange angry words. And Tom hears Linda say the word "jail." He says this triggers his attack because his mother had once threatened his father with jail for not providing support money.

Tom holds a kitchen knife at Linda's heart and stabs her, he told police. Then he saw that she was suffering and he didn't want that, so he kept stabbing.

Afterwards, he kisses his sleeping kids, writes his note, takes pills and calls police.

The police call comes in at 12:27 a.m. It is noted there is a child crying in the background. It is the two-year-old.

Tom told the dispatcher, "I have taken an overdose and hurt my wife."

Three separate times during the short call, Tom begs police to not let the children see their mother. He says, "Please, don't let my kids see it." And finally, "Help my kids."

In his many mental health interviews, Tom has complaints about Linda. The immediate problem is Linda is the "bread winner," he says. He adds, "My wife was always sloppy. She changed when she went to work. She combed her hair." He thought Linda is becoming less attentive and affectionate. And he is "agitated and suspicious" about the recent marriage counseling to which Linda has taken him. One psychologist concludes Tom has "possessive and domineering attitudes towards his wife."

After the judge sentenced Tom in October 1975 and he is returned to a state hospital, Tom's mental state improves quickly. By January 1976, he is granted ground privileges.

That fall, he is admitted to the Seagull Individual Living Program. This is described in one report as having "cottage life and programs." Tom is also given weekend passes from the state hospital so he can visit his mother and children. And he even lives in a nearby Youngstown halfway house for a few months in 1978.

In April 1979, he has a hearing to decide whether he is still mentally ill or not. His family hires their own psychologists and those findings are that "any return to jail, even for a brief period, would likely precipitate a relapse into active psychosis."

Tom's career goals are by then to be a plumber or electrician, or a golf pro at a country club.

So it is concluded that psychotropic drugs, treatment at a community mental health center and enrollment in a psychotherapy program are what Tom needs.

The court of common pleas disagrees. And on April 20, 1979, Tom is declared "mentally ill and returned to the custody of the department of mental retardation for further treatment."

Another competency hearing is scheduled for May 30, 1980 but Tom dies a few weeks before, on May 18.

He never serves any prison time. Doctors and lawyers establish that Tom's brain is unhinged. After spending his time in a quiet sanatorium or "cottage life," his mental health improves but not enough so he stays in the system. His dream of a golf pro job at a country club remains on hold. But then, there's his death.

It takes me four straight hours to read all this. I develop a pounding headache. But before I can gather up my notebook and purse and flee this paper scene of a murder, I want to hear a deposition I gave. I borrow a tape recorder, retreat to a private office and hear my blinders-on, limited version of how Linda met her death.

Chapter Six
Inside Scoop on the Crime

As I mull over these memories and rich history, still in Akron in 1989, it's time to hear from Linda's family. I wake up the next day at 7 a.m. after reading all these files but it isn't until 10 a.m. that I call Linda's mother.

But first, I call Margaret Garforth, who worked in the PGA office with us. She handled Carter's dictation – an honest-to-goodness secretary unlike Linda and me, like I said.

She called me a "smartass kid" back then. I cherish that label a lot.

After talking about the shock of Linda's death, she says, "I remember how much I hated that job. (Boss) Carter's snorting in the morning made my stomach queasy."

Margaret is married to her high school sweetheart, Raymond, who sells furniture at nearby O'Neil's department store. She scoots out a lot for lunch with her husband. So day after day, it's just Linda and me at noon. We seldom buy our lunch, both dreading when Carter is in town so we can't commence our chitchatting. And I know I'll be making the hot dog run if Carter is there.

Margaret remembers the volunteer gala we were invited to for the kick-off of the PGA Championship. It is held in August 1975 at Firestone Country Club with drinks and nibbles. No major golf players but we feel like the help (us) is let out of the kitchen. There we are in our finery, finally meeting all these people on all the committees and most every hotshot in our rubber plant town.

I wear a blue dress my mother has sewn which has a large sequin butterfly on the front. Margaret and I remember Linda especially that night – how this party would have been everything in the world for her.

After Linda's death, she is replaced by a mousy-looking woman wearing a brown wig. I make no attempt to get friendly but Margaret finds out why her wig is askew every day by 5. She's taking Valium, Margaret tells me, trying to cope with having a child late in life. She doesn't show up for work one day and that is the end of that. So leading up to the tournament, we have another woman on staff, Dorothy Graham, who's nice and competent. I can't help but warm up to her because she's a pleasure to be around.

In 1989, Margaret is 67 with diabetes and two open heart surgeries. But she has a commendable career after her PGA job. In the small world of Akron, she takes a temp job at Kelley Girls and is sent to the same building where our PGA office was located. As it turns out, she works at the same law firm that had donated our PGA space. The firm then hires her within two days of her temp work and she works for five years for a lawyer who has the *Beacon Journal* as one of its clients.

Margaret believes Linda waited too long for help. I expect her to say this. But then she adds that Linda also needed help to understand why she put up with Tom for so long. I'm not ready to sort out that aspect quite yet.

Exactly 14 years after Linda Mae (Spring) McLain is laid to rest in Rose Hill cemetery, I sit in her mother and stepfather's living room in Akron. Both Genevieve Jones and her husband Kinzer, nickname of Ken, whom she married after Linda graduated from high school in 1965, are pleasant looking, friendly and candid.

Genevieve says exactly what's on her mind and Kinzer, while more introspective, comes across as a nice guy, the kind who would drive Linda and her friends anywhere they asked, as Genevieve tells me, as he did years before marrying her mom.

They live in a modest home, nothing fancy but cozy. Genevieve has outright contempt for the memory of Tom; Kinzer keeps quiet on that grievous issue and talks most about the rough life Linda had as Mrs. McLain.

Genevieve tells me Tom committed suicide. "Thank God he did," she says. But her version of how he dies doesn't make sense to me. She tells me that Tom, out on one of his weekend passes from the mental hospital, went up to a local tavern, got drunk and then went home to his mother's house and overdosed on pills.

The date this happened is an anniversary of Linda's birthday.

But Tom isn't a drinker, I'm thinking. His blood analysis after Linda's murder shows phenobarbital and Tranxene, both depressants, but no alcohol.

And is he really out on the town, in his mother's care, with that much freedom? I can't believe such a thing.

I don't voice these questions but I do tell her mother I want so much to write about domestic violence and my

PGA friend. I'm thinking that information about Tom's demise will be uncovered as I do further research.

Genevieve tells me she is divorced from Linda's dad when Linda is two. She devotes herself to raising her child. She says she even kept Kinzer on the string, in a five- or six-year courtship, waiting to marry him when Linda is out of high school.

The two women are buddies. Linda wrote her mother a letter later in life saying she missed their long talks, Genevieve says. Kinzer shows me photo albums. He keeps everything in neat order, even the receipt for Linda's gravestone.

Linda is shapely and beautiful in high school. She is on the Winter Wonderland dance court. She dates a "handsome minister's son," her mom recalls of happier times.

Then Linda is given a car and Genevieve and Ken both agree "she went a little wild." She starts hanging out at the Pogo restaurant, the burger place where she meets Tom.

Within months after graduating from high school, Linda is begging her mother to sign for her so she could marry Tom. Genevieve refuses. She doesn't like the dark and gloomy Tom and she feels Linda, who is 18, is too young to get married.

But then friends and family convince her that with Tom's family's money, the couple can easily drive to Michigan and be married where it isn't necessary to have a parent's signature if you're under 21.

I handle a few wedding snapshots of Tom and Linda. They had children, moved around a lot and sometimes

Linda came home for money and rest, but always without Tom. He isn't welcome.

Genevieve says that Tom didn't financially support Linda. But she also knows about the physical abuse. She would notice Linda with a swollen eye or bruises on her arms.

In 1970, Linda is in intensive care in a local hospital. Genevieve had no idea what is wrong with her daughter, who is running a high fever. "Then the Sanginiti's family doctor (Tom's stepfather had hired him), told me about the infection that had set in on Linda's arm."

Genevieve says Linda won't tell her about the injury right away, then finally she confesses that Tom had hit her with a golf club. It is a bad bruise that has become infected.

Why didn't Genevieve do something to stop this abuse? She tells me that for seven of the eight years Linda is married, she does nothing but plead with Linda to leave her husband. "Then one night, I was laying in bed bawling my eyes out, and Ken came in and said, 'Gen, you've been doing it this way and it's not working. Now try another way. Keep quiet. Don't say a word to Linda about Tom. Talk about everything else.'"

A heart-broken mother takes his advice. One story Genevieve tells me is particularly upsetting. Linda would go to her mother's house and wait with the kids to pick up Tom from his factory job at 10 p.m.

This disturbed Genevieve because her grandkids are up so late on school nights. "I always told Linda she needed a schedule for those kids. She was always in bed at their age by 8:30."

This hits me so hard because when Linda worked with me at the PGA, she took the bus to and from work. This is even after Tom is laid-off and is at home with the car. One night, Linda misses the bus, and comes back into the office to thaw out before the next bus arrives. Her legs are frozen blue because this Ohio winter of our PGA job is brutal. I give her a lift home.

The Joneses have photos of the children in their living room. I see their mother's features in Scott, Jody and Kara. James Miller, Genevieve's brother-in-law, took the children. At the time of the homicide, Miller is comfortably ensconced in the executive suite at General Tire and he and his wife, Eva, live in a spacious house with their two grown children off to college.

Genevieve says after Linda's funeral, she has to stay with Kinzer's relatives in Florida for six months to deal with her grief. Soon after, she takes a medical disability from her job at General Tire, and says she has a myriad of health problems now at age 64.

Not long after Linda's death, the three children have contact with their father. This deeply disturbs Genevieve. But Tom is dead now and the tragedy Genevieve calls "a mess from the word go" is continuing but on a slower pace. Tom's mother, Patricia Sanginiti, dies at age 61 in 1984 and his stepfather, Dominic Sanginiti, dies at age 71 in 1985.

The Sanginiti money Genevieve hopes would keep Linda afloat in her young, hasty marriage, instead keeps Tom out of jail.

Genevieve is vague about how the details of Linda's death have been presented to the children. She hints that she's somewhat on-the-outs with her sister and brother-in-law because they allowed so much contact between Tom and Scott, Jody and Kara.

Mrs. Miller, who is on a vacation cruise with her husband when I am in Akron, refuses to be interviewed for my *St. Petersburg Times* story when I reach her later on the telephone.

Genevieve provides these brief details about the kids. The youngest, Kara, now 15, is a high school sophomore, who attends church regularly and is very smart in school. Scott is 22 and about to graduate from Ohio State. He's athletic, in a fraternity and does visit the Joneses when he's home on vacations. Genevieve also says he has expressed an interest in knowing about his mother and went down to the *Beacon Journal* to see what he could find out.

Jody, 21, graduated from high school but has dropped out of Genevieve's life. She later lived with the Sanginitis and then a friend of theirs intermittently after the death of her parents.

But Genevieve is prepared if any of the children want answers some day. Kinzer has made up a set of color photographs of Linda for each of the McLain children, and so far, only Kara has claimed them.

Before I leave, I offer a gift. It is a sterling silver necklace in its original box. This jewelry is given to each of the staff and volunteers who worked the PGA. I believe this is our bonus. The chain holds a big square insignia with crossed blue and green painted golf clubs. I hope Genevieve will give my tournament necklace to one of Linda's children.

After my chat with the Joneses, I need to know the details of Tom's death. The 1980 coroner's report about the day Tom died with $10.86 in his pocket at his mother's Akron home is straightforward. It mentions he tries to hang himself in jail a week after the murder. And that one doctor treats him for schizophrenia, chronic undifferentiated type.

Herbert David McLain is a widower, unemployed (mental patient). From my calculations, he gains about 40 pounds in those five years from Linda's death.

His death is ruled a suicide due to ingestion of barbiturates, no alcohol is found in his blood.

His mother states in the report that on May 16, 1980 (Linda would have been 33), she picks Tom up at the Massillon State Hospital for a weekend visit. Tom appears despondent, Mrs. Sanginiti states, and he tells her that he never wants to go back to the state hospital again.

She calls her son for dinner at 7:30 and he says he loves her but is too tired to eat. She checks on him about midnight and he is asleep. At 10 the next morning, Tom is found dead in his bed by his mother, and is pronounced DOA at 11:35 a.m. at Akron City Hospital.

That is that. No partying at the end, at least.

As for that tape-recorded deposition I gave a few months after Linda's death, I think about that a lot as I mentally organize what I'm learning. Dated April 9, 1975, it is very, very eerie to hear my voice from 14 years earlier. I was a kid with two kids back then, fueled by vodka and tonics and Kool menthol cigarettes. Carter, my PGA boss, doesn't want me to give this deposition but I get involved anyway.

Carter would never have been a comfort in regards to Linda's murder. He displayed almost annoyance as host of this upcoming PGA party that he could be linked with something so anti-social as a murder. He continued to make comments about our "hick town." Our office failed to close the day of Linda's death. And later, she received no mention in the PGA book.

Right after the murder, I leave some toys at Linda's parents' house for Scott, Jody and Kara with money collected in our tournament office. But I don't go to the private funeral nor does anyone else at the PGA office. I am too much of an emotional mess – I don't know about the others. Plus, I really avoid funerals since more than 10 years earlier my 21-year-old cousin was killed by a drunk driver coming home from a Cleveland Indians baseball game.

Back to my deposition (I had to sneak out of the office to give this), when the prosecutor asks me for a final observation, I say, "She was really crazy about this guy (Tom)."

The prosecutor replies, "And he was probably really crazy."

Chapter Seven
Orphans in Ohio

Now please jump ahead to 1998. Ten years later, my life is again moving toward being settled. After leaving the *St. Petersburg Times* for the *Des Moines Register* where I again bump into Oprah when she's in Iowa for the Bridges of Madison County saga, I'm back in Florida briefly working as a stringer for the *St. Petersburg Times*. I land at the *Tampa Tribune* in January 1997. As I said, I marry photographer Ray Bassett in 1995 and we live in a condominium on an island, Tierra Verde, near the Sunshine Skyway bridge where fresh air blows in from the Gulf of Mexico.

In 1998, I'm wondering what happens long term to children when a father murders the mother. This is a crime too ghastly to believe by adults, let alone fully comprehended by children. So many of these domestic violence stories are in the news, ending with the kids shipped off to relatives.

I am curious about this because I have a relationship with Mabel Bexley who runs The Spring, Florida's largest certified domestic violence shelter system. Located in Tampa, The Spring is hidden in an urban neighborhood. Bexley offers my daughter and me a tour one day where we see an indoor tent city-like set up. Women and their children have claimed a corner of space with their possessions. I bring up the subject of the little victims of domestic violence. She says the studies are new in this area but time and therapy would certainly help.

Bexley (who retired in 2002 at age 65), often mentions that Linda's maiden name is Spring. She urges me to pursue what happened to Scott, Jody and Kara and maybe I will come away with some insight. "Images of mommy and daddy fighting follow children into their dreams," says Bexley, looking like a doting grandmother with her tiny white hair bun. "Children blame themselves for the violence. They long to be safe at home."

Maybe I could go to Akron on some vacation time. But that doesn't work out. I get close though. I travel to Michigan for the birth of my first grandchild. In August 1998, Jack Ryan Froelich is born but with pneumonia and is in intensive care for a week. So all my vacation time is spent worrying about his welfare.

Despite this upheaval of events, I still have an interest in Genevieve Jones and how she continues to cope in the aftermath of Linda's murder.

As for the kids, I know they went to a rich relative. But now they are ages 31, 30 and 25. I never mailed Linda's mother a copy of my story. It ran in 1989. It is a condensed version of all my notes. I want mostly to run a big box with phone numbers for help in domestic violence situations. The *St. Petersburg Times* does this.

But I don't want Linda's mother to read the disturbing suicide note Tom left. He sits down (next to the body?) and writes about loving a gal named Shirley right after he murders Linda. My thinking is Linda's mom is too fragile to read this and the contents of the note, of course, are in my story.

But I could call Genevieve even if my Akron visit is a wash because I needed to get back to work. After a few cups of coffee, I dial Linda's mother. It's been three years since I last checked in with her. I have breezy conversations once in awhile and this is how I learn Linda's children have all graduated college.

No one answers and I'm sort of relieved. This is so difficult; the tension sizzles under my armpits. Later in the afternoon, I call and a sleepy sounding Genevieve answers. Her voice shakes off the effects of a nap quickly. She begins by telling me Linda would have been 51. "Every birthday, I say, 'Happy birthday, honey, wherever you are right now.'"

Genevieve reflects, "If you lose a child, no matter if six months or six years passes, you never get over it."

We talk and I sense a new connection – perhaps because I'm long out of that young category. I'm 52, I tell her, and that seems to make her comfortable.

Genevieve gives me lengthy backgrounds of the children. Their lives sound busy. Kara earns a degree from Kent State in 1997, my alma mater. She also lived in Beall Hall, the same dormitory where I dwelled for a spell. She married Mark Wilson last December 1997.

"Both Mark (Kara's husband) and Kara are the babies of the family," Genevieve says with great satisfaction. She sounds uplifted talking about how vivacious Kara is and how quiet Mark is.

Kara teaches at the Interfaith Family Elementary School in downtown Akron. She teaches 22 children.

She brings her small dog to school and the children get to play with the pup during the noon hour. On Sunday, she's a waitress at an Egg Castle. Her husband has a year or two to go on his degree and he's transferred from Kent State to University of Akron. He works part-time at a bike shop and the two are bartenders at special events and parties.

Genevieve says the young couple pick her and her husband up and bring them over to their apartment for supper once in awhile. This sounds so special to Genevieve.

She says Kara has the dark eyes and hair of "you know who," her way of dismissing Tom's existence. "She looks a lot like her mother too with her high cheek bones," she adds.

She has fewer details about Scott but she remarks that he and his wife, Molly, are just dying for her and Kinzer to come down to Columbus where they live for a visit. "I've had a very ill husband for the last four or five years, "sighs Genevieve. "So we don't go much of anywhere."

Scott has a master's from Ohio State in sports medicine. He lived in Chicago but after his August 1995 marriage in Akron, he moved back to Columbus where the cost of living is cheaper. "He wanted to be around his old fraternity buddies too," says his grandmother.

Genevieve dearly loves all her grandchildren. She's a little concerned about Jody having a baby so young in life without a husband. But then having a child out of wedlock would be an old-fashioned worry.

Genevieve first says Jody doesn't have any connection to the Millers and then later in our conversation she says the couple sometimes take Jody's 10-year-old son to Sunday School. Jody works two jobs, including as a social worker. She graduated from the University of Akron.

As for the Millers, they live half the year in Naples, Fla., the other in Akron. Genevieve talks as if the relationship with her sister has improved. Things were strained because Eva allowed Tom to visit his children.

Now Genevieve says she makes a list of everything she wants to ask Eva because their time together is so short – with the Millers being in Florida a lot. "She took me to the store the other day," says Genevieve. "But I didn't get to ask her everything because she was in such a hurry."

The Millers are both 71. This means they were 48 when they took in the McLain children. They celebrated their 50th wedding anniversary on May 28 with a 10-day cruise, sailing from New York. "It's old stuff to them," says Genevieve, who adds the pair have traveled the globe since Miller's retirement from General Tire in 1985.

Genevieve adores "Jimmy," something I have not heard her say before. "It's been a God's blessing he got those children," she says, explaining how he set aside Social Security money for their college and offered them down payment funds for homes if they worked hard and finished college in due time.

"He's just like an old shoe," she says of Miller, who also has a place in Myrtle Beach where Genevieve says she and her husband are welcome to winter if it weren't for Kinzer's poor health.

She says Miller makes pie crust. She laughs at how weird this sounds. It is funny to think about something quirky regarding an old mainline rubber company executive, one of a stuffy bunch who dressed uniformly in white shirts and dark suits back when Akron was the Tire Capital of the World.

"He's been good to us," she says, half-sad. Before she hangs up, she says she'd like me to meet Kara. Hopefully, I can make it to Akron sometime but my daughter is getting married in November. Kara is special because I remember Tom carrying the toddler into the PGA office; Kara was dressed in a pink blanket snow suit.

I call Cathy Tierney at the *Beacon Journal* so she can read me Kara's wedding announcement. She does so. It appeared in the newspaper Dec. 28, 1997. The groom's name is Mark Lincoln Wilson. The bride's full name is Kara Jene McLain. It sounds like a big church wedding, held at Westminster Presbyterian. The reception is a cake and punch affair in the social hall.

As I'm mentally sniffing lily of the valley and roses, Cathy reads a line from the announcement that causes me to pause. "Could you read me that again?" I ask. Kara Jene McLain is the niece of Eva and James Miller and Mark Lincoln Wilson is the son of Lois and Peter Wilson.

That's it. Linda's existence isn't recorded in the tapestry of this fancy wedding for her beloved youngest daughter. No mention of the mother.

Jody McLain is the maid of honor.

Hearing this I'm having a flashback of Linda. She has on those darn high heels Eva gave her – the ones she hides in her desk drawer so Tom doesn't know about them. She loved the way the shoes played up the shape of her legs. She'd try them on, stick out her leg and tense the calf muscle and then walk around in them with the confidence of a good-looking woman.

Linda existed all right.

I pull a few public records (called an auto track which shows driver license information) at the *Tampa Tribune* on the three McLain children and see that their eye and hair color are a checkerboard of their parents. Scott has reddish brown hair and hazel eyes. Jody has brown hair, blue eyes and Kara has brown hair, brown eyes.

Chapter Eight
Jogging Memories

Finally, we reach present day. Maybe I had a premonition that I would soon have time on my hands. But right before I was laid off at the *Tampa Tribune*, nine days before I turned 62 in July 2008, I did some online searches for the McLain children.

This took some effort but by the end of my search I had where all three are plus two photos to ponder – of Scott and Kara.

Right away, I came up with an obituary for James H. Miller, who died at age 80 on Oct. 16, 2007. He was not only high up in General Tire but also in the community.

He held an MBA from University of Akron and worked at General Tire for 33 years. There he was vice president of Chemical/Plastics Division, president of the Tire Division and retired as vice president of Administration. He was on lots of boards of directors, Banc Ohio, National City Bank, Davey Tree, Akron General Medical Center and Ohio Presbyterian Retirement Services.

He was a member of Portage Country Club and First Presbyterian Church.

He was married to Eva for 59 years. His children are listed as a daughter and son, and the three McLains.

"Jim Miller was very conservative in everything he did," says Ed Kalail, who retired in 1995 from General Tire after 32 years in public relations. "So for him to take those children in was really something."

As an executive at General Tire, Kalail says Miller was known as a "fine gentleman. He didn't have a mean bone in his body." In other words, he was the acme of respectability.

In continuing my research, I find Scott McLain online easily. He's club manager at One Eleven Fitness Club on South Wacker in Chicago and runs a fitness boot camp in Columbus and Chicago. Kara lives in Greensboro, N.C. and has two daughters. She won a chili cook-off contest in her subdivision.

Jody is tougher to find although I see something online about her son, Sebastian Hopson, who played football at Firestone High School. Then I remember to read the guest book for Miller's obit and find out Jody works for Summit County Children's Services in the Kinship Department.

Miller's son, Dr. David Miller, isn't a physician. The guest book indicates he's a minister. I find out quickly he preaches in Peachtree, Ga. I e-mail him at his First Presbyterian Church because I figure he would be a good family spokesperson but fail to get a response. I wonder if he has ever preached about his unique blended family. The daughter, Sandy, founded a sign company, Signmaster Inc., in Lewis Center, Ohio in 1997. She's married to Michael Beetner, an advocate for Parkinson's disease sufferers.

I take a break from the death notice and look up Firestone Country Club online and find there are now three courses and 15 condominium villas associated with the still private club. There's also a public nine-hole course. I also look up the 1894-founded, Tudor-style Portage Country Club, looking as regal as ever.

I call Dale Antram, easily located online at Mercury Luggage in Jacksonville. He says he left the *Beacon Journal* as a sports writer in 1969 – must have been right before I started at the newspaper because I don't recall this part of his resume. Then he joins Firestone public relations, works the 57th Championship and then scoots out of Akron in 1979 to work for the PGA of America in Florida.

He says Firestone Country Club (he recalls off the top of his head that it is founded in 1929 by Harvey Firestone) is sold in 1981 to ClubCorp out of Dallas. At the time, he says, "Everyone thought this was a foolish decision."

But the company put in the villas at the west end of the 667-yards long 16th hole and turned the country club into a resort operation. This probably saves Firestone from a downward spiral because Antram says golf changed, requiring bigger courses and the expansions aren't cheap. Also bigger holes – Firestone's 16th hole is now 667-yards long; whereas, in Nicklaus' PGA winning days, he recalls in his book it was 625 yards.

Antram is foggy on the memory of Linda's murder so I will send him the obit to jog his memory. As for Ed Carter, Antram, always the polished professional, says only, "He was an amazing character," with eyebrow lifting in his voice.

We are not alone in this opinion. The *SI* article I referred to earlier, calls Carter "the only true impresario the tour ever had." *SI* reports he was a showman who knew how to squeeze the last dollar out of pro golf. He's also called ebullient, which means boiling, agitated. Good thing, I served Carter those wieners promptly.

The way Antram explains how the tournament was run back in 1975 is the PGA of America – representing those who play golf for a living such as teachers and club pros – ran the tournaments but couldn't afford full time directors. So they hired Ed Carter ("J. Edwin Carter," Antram corrects my casually calling him "Ed" and laughs). It's just been in the last 20 or so years that the PGA has a staff person as championship director.

"Back then, the tournaments mostly went to courses that had existing structures of volunteers. It was very easy to come to Firestone." He recalls the club even pinch-hits in 1960 for Cherry Creek C.C. when that course is flooded and has to close for a year.

Golf courses had to reinvent themselves to meet the athleticism of today's golfer. Firestone, always well-manicured, had to have even firmer fairways. Greens had to have tighter conditions where shots could bounce and roll. Antram says today's golfer thinks nothing of shooting 280 to 320 yards with abandonment, knowing he or she will make up precision on the greens.

The press tent at the 1975 PGA tournament – which Antram is basically in charge of – housed about 50 reporters from major newspapers and news outlets plus all the Ohio and surrounding states' sports crews. But still, the sport then is peanuts monetarily. Johnny Miller is the leader in money winning standings in all of 1974 at $353,021 followed by Jack Nicklaus at $238,178. In 2008, Padraig Harrington earns $1.35 million just for winning the PGA Championship alone.

Antram was just in Ohio for a wedding and his twin brother lives in Tampa. He says what he remembers most about the 57th PGA is that Bruce Crampton shot a record low 63 on the second round. Antram still has a photo of the golfer, who lost that squeaker to Nicklaus in the end, posing with his brother and him right after that spectacular round. It's funny to talk so easily to someone from so long ago. I remember Antram as a bespectacled guy with dark sideburns and slick back hair. He was the steady go-to guy, not a bit moody or grumpy like Carter. I'm sure those qualities served him well at the PGA where he worked for 22 years for PGA Commissioner Deane Beman.

Linda's murder received scant attention in the press. Today, her association with the PGA may have caught the fancy of the 24/7 media. Focus on these cases caused a change in attitude about domestic violence eventually.

But I'm still curious about if there is anything in the way of a lasting memorial for her. I don't really know what I mean by that but I'll recognize it when I see it. Does Linda Spring McLain have any kind of legacy? As for her children, I feel a massive wave of sadness that their tenuous memories of their mother may have faded. The youngest, Kara, may have had nothing to hang on to at all.

I thought for sure Emily Petrarca, chairman of the women's committee for the 57th PGA Championship, would remember the murder of Linda. Emily, who always looked athletic and wore her hair in a swinging blonde bob, is reached at her Akron home. She doesn't remember.

I will fax her the newspaper clippings. Emily, explaining she's been having some problems with an unexplained weight loss, says Richard Guster lives in her neighborhood. She sees him walking. He was the head honcho of the tournament, the one Carter was always nice to. I will reach him for sure. I hope I don't keep running into more faded memories. But hey, when you call people out of the blue and say, "Remember 30-some years ago when..."

With her health problems, could Linda's mother Genevieve still be around? I call the number I have and a younger sounding man is on the answering machine.

It takes a few days of this but meanwhile, I find a few Christmas cards she's sent me from 2000 on. The first, she wrote: "So sorry to tell you Ken has been in a nursing home." The second that Kinzer had died at age 82 of diabetes and congestive heart failure after having his leg amputated. The next card she signs simply, "Love Genevieve Jones." Then – and this gets interesting – in 2004 it's greetings from Robert and Genevieve Miller.

Miller???? I would have dropped the card in the snow, only I live in Florida. I try calling her back then but no answer and I'm whisked away into daily life.

"I've buried two husbands in six years. Guess I won't try that again," booms Genevieve Miller on the phone in July 2008. It seems as Kinzer is dying at the nursing home, she meets the man in the next room tending to his ill spouse. The Miller name, same as her brother-in-law and sister, is just a coincidence.

There's bad news for Scott. He and his wife Molly divorce after eight years of marriage, says Genevieve.

Kara's two girls are little dolls. And Jody remains in Akron.

Kinzer is clearly on her mind. They were married for 37 years and he dies in 2001. Her latest husband dies nine days before James Miller, the General Tire honcho who's her brother-in-law. They are married for three years and had bought a Uniontown condominium together in Spring Water Gardens.

They were having furniture moved in when her husband took ill. Now she's trying to sell because she's decided to stay in her house where she's lived for 54 years.

As for the Millers, Genevieve said unlike most seniors, the couple decide to buy a new house when they are in their seventies.

Now sadly James Miller is gone but Eva is as busy as ever, playing bridge and golfing at Portage Country Club. She still winters in Naples.

"I don't see my sister much," says Genevieve, who's 84. "I still drive so I go to the store and drive myself around. Anything to not sit here with too much time on my hands."

I'm learning about time on my hands. Through trial and error, falsehood and my own silly foolishness, right one time and wrong the next, inspired but scared, I decide to go all the way down memory lane and look closer at how my life unfolds after the PGA Championship and my encounter with Linda's death.

When I left that golf job, I systemically implode my life in Akron as I know it. Maybe it is because of the lack of a scream. The morning I walked into the PGA office and found out Linda had been brutally murdered by Tom, I went totally inward. I didn't wail or duck into the staircase for a loud outcry. I simply continued on as any good Akronite does because holding on to a paycheck is the Midwestern way for sanity.

Chapter Nine
To the Manor Born

As a young woman, I am a quasi-Ohio housewife and my great pleasure in life is a Burger King Whopper. It is messy and requires many napkins for all the beef juice and mustard drippings. I love my children dearly but I am so restless that it's amazing sneaking away in the afternoon for a large burger calms me down. I do tend to comfort myself with food, even today.

Drugs and alcohol never serve me as reliable companions.

As for drinking, blame the built-in stop device in my head where vomiting and headache are triggered for days afterwards. When I have more than two drinks, the world is a grand and funny place. But then I start slurring my words. The worst part of this is I can hear myself with the run-on sentences – most unattractive. Alcoholic Anonymous is founded in Akron in 1935 so that's one part of my heritage I'll pass on.

Ideally, I don't want to soothe my disappointments or numb myself against the world with alcohol. But the ideal life escapes most everyone I know. And I do have a hate horror of driving drunk. My husband is happy to be married to a designated driver.

Back in Akron, my dream is to leave town and do something creative with my life. This isn't an explosive intensity ambition. I really just like learning new things. Then in a textured story, I relay them to readers. It is a basic drive. I enjoy a different challenge all the time.

I am greatly influenced by the women's liberation movement. With a history of half the population in servitude – that's a compelling reason to get riled up. Akron is a grand place to get all feminist - Soujourner Truth delivered her "Ain't I A Woman" speech in Akron in 1851 at the Ohio Women's Rights Convention.

I always had this notion that women should plow forward in relationships. I propose to Larry in the fall of 1967 when we are circling a round-about in suburban Tallmadge with our song, the Beach Boys' "Wouldn't It Be Nice" on the radio.

When I cover a few national protest demonstrations for the Equal Rights Amendment for the *Beacon Journal,* I am surrounded by gutsy women who don't want to be told this is correct and this isn't. It seems the media is focused on their not shaving legs and armpits. In any case, utmost respectability bites the dust from this movement. I relish that down to my toes.

The magic of the women's lib movement works on me but not because I'm denied most professional opportunities. I am editor of the *Daily Kent Stater* my senior year in spring 1968. And while I am shuffled off to the women's department at the *Beacon Journal* in 1969 to write some wedding and engagement stories, I like this job because I want steady 9 to 5 hours what with my son, Mark, a toddler. This is my choice.

Anyway, I feel in over-my-head typing my first story at this newspaper. Larry helps me with the interview of an Episcopal priest who has a hand-carved crèche on display in his Akron church. This is the historical St. Andrew's Episcopal where I am later baptized in May 1981. I must have felt gratitude my career started out okay.

I am a very green cub-ette reporter where the larger-than-life John S. Knight lumbers down the halls and writes his award-winning "Editor's Notebook."

I am 23 with a one-year-old son. Women work there and at other newspapers but mostly women are known as sob sisters or women's department staffers. Some of my female co-workers are single or had raised their kids. But the newspaper gives me at least a half dozen solid role models who represent professional women – a species I'm not really that familiar with. These include Joan Rice, Fran Murphy, Pat Ravenscraft, Nancy Yockey, who had earlier helped me land a KSU scholarship, Pat Dunphy and finally, Polly Paffilias, who good-naturedly chides the kid in me.

I am in heaven. I want to be a journalist since the sixth grade. The pit bull editor Ben Maidenburg isn't charmed, however. I am hired by the enthusiastic young managing editor Bob Giles (he's served as the curator of the Nieman Foundation for Journalists at Harvard University since 2000).

But Maidenburg causes me grief from the beginning. My schedule is to work four week days and then on Saturday come in and write those nuptial doings. This way Larry and I only need a babysitter for only four days.

One Saturday when Maidenburg and I are among the few in the office, he growls at skinny me eating a Twinkie, "Who the hell's at home, feeding that kid of yours?"

I answer, "No one." He doesn't get the joke. Anti-working mom and a swift carrier of exploding expletives are his trademarks, in my mind.

As if I need proof of how provincial Maidenburg is, he comes down on me like a bat-out-of-hell when I write an article criticizing O'Neil's department store for including car coats in a fashion show.

As a young person, I want to give a kick to the establishment and Maidenburg is the polar opposite. He's a booster for his community, heavy on society affairs.

But I don't fret. I am living my dream. And having a giggle too. My boss is Betty Jaycox. Her BJ monogram as in *Beacon Journal* or her name (cute, huh?) is on everything she wears. This is before ethics codes are enforced at newspapers and Betty or BJ has me toting her wigs up to Polsky's for a free wash and set. She also buys designers' clothes at cost when she travels to write about the New York City fashion shows. I stay put, covering trunk shows at Polsky's and O'Neil's.

But BJ writes hundreds of stories in a smooth conversational style that wins her many awards and a huge following. She writes endlessly about the joys of the lakeside "Half Day Farm" out in Springfield. But I'm never invited to her house. I enjoy her columns because she just plain puts her nose in everybody's business while bragging about her country life and great career. What a gal! She also has great boldness. Men, even Maidenburg, walk on egg shells around her.

"Betty was very intimidating," says Giles, 76, during a recent phone call from his Cambridge, Mass., office. His voice sounds as if it is shaking at the memory on the phone. "She had that great power in her column. It was a must-read in Akron," he says.

"It was a way for people to hear the gossip about the Portage Country Club set," Giles adds, saying Jack Knight and Betty Jaycox loved the social scene whereas Ben Maidenburg was a stay-at-home when not working.

Jaycox, who wore false eyelashes everyday to the office, liked to dress me down for not dressing up. She takes me aside one day and bluntly blurts out, "You and Larry are both working now. You should dress better." She inspires me to buy a bright red skirt, short of course, white blouse, navy pantyhose and red, white and blue bead necklace. I wear this on many assignments. It is my conservative look.

I also enjoy my work for the *Beacon's* Sunday magazine, and continue that even after my full-time job is over. Newspapers don't offer these magazines much any more but it's an opportunity to write some offbeat stuff. After the PGA tournament in 1976, for my story about "Who's Who on Merriman Road?" about the richest street in town where the rubber swells live, I pull out my PGA Izod dress, shortened but still presentable. This is for a normal look I wish to create as I knock on mansion doors.

As the first person in a large blue-collar family to go to college, I learn that a woman getting a fair share of unfairness in a lopsided world is about all that can be expected. But I always want fun in the equation too.

My husband respects me but he never really says this to others: "Janis thinks this..." so common in close marriages. I can be silly but my wit isn't trigger quick like Larry's. For too long, he is the leader, I am the follower.

I had my son the day I graduated from college. I planned to graduate in June 1968 but then I screw up, reading a Muhammad Ali *Vanity Fair* profile and other pop culture stories instead of knuckling down to pass French. I must waddle, heavy and pregnant, to summer school to take one solo French class. Hence I go into labor shortly before "Pomp and Circumstances" fills the Kent State auditorium. My college degree is then brought to the hospital on that Aug. 31, 1968 day when my son Mark is born.

Larry doesn't share my zest of being a goof off. I want an adventure or two. I want to hit the highway of self-discovery. But I can't budge him from Akron. He views his job as financial security, the anchor for our family. Immaturity is my style. I don't want routine. I have all these confusing thoughts when I should be enjoying the Kent home with the kiddies and hubby. Larry buys me Villager clothes for Christmas. What more could a wife ask for?

I don't want to say our marriage busting up is because of the cultural times. The 1970s are no rougher on marriages than any other era fraught with discord which is every decade in American history.

The newsroom is a rough place for relationships, though. The long hours and tension of always being on top of a story hurt people needing to be home for supper. Plus, this is the place winning a Pulitzer Prize in 1971 for general reporting of the Kent State shootings. Many reporters are either continuing coverage of that earth-shattering day, May 4, 1970, or off to new careers because of the plumped up resumes.

Larry and I hang out with the newspaper crowd and watch marriage after marriage crumble. I know from the courtship that Larry is smartly confident and I am a jumble of insecurities. But we have two lovely children we both adore and care for. Larry, an Ohio University graduate who served as a lieutenant in the Army, has a family-centered upbringing as much as I do.

I grew up behind a Firestone burning tire dump on the outskirts of Akron. This explains my desire to this day of wanting to live some place sans air pollution. Larry, dark and handsome with an engaging smile, had a Beaver Cleaver childhood in Dover, about an hour's drive from Akron. In the 1970s, his parents live in Orrville, home of Smucker's where life is certainly sticky endearing in a jelly milieu.

But the immunities of youth and prettiness offer little immunity after all. From the PGA job on, the marriage falls apart.

Chapter Ten
Separate but Equal

Larry and I hammer out a formal separation agreement in 1981. I saved a card from that time that Larry wrote to me. He is so good at summarizing but then he's been a top editor for years. He retired from the *Lexington Herald Leader* in Kentucky as news editor and continued to work part-time until age 68.

Larry writes: "I guess the last two nights are typical of the inner torture I've been wrestling with. Going out with you on Tuesday to a quiet restaurant and talking was an exceptional luxury for me – and maybe for you, too.

"But then tonight. There you sat, all perfumed and in a sexy dress watching our children play. I knew you were headed elsewhere for the rest of the evening and couldn't bear the thought of you with another man –'people' you say. I just can't handle that aspect of this relationship. I know only too well I'm applying a double standard when I act and feel that way. But there are emotions that drive their way into my consciousness and make it impossible for me to say, 'Well, she's not doing anything that I'm not doing.' I recognize that, but can't cope with it.

"That's why dissolving this marriage must go ahead as soon as possible. You talk about sorting our feelings, what a mess we've made of things, and how you're still not sure this is what you want to do. But your actions – and mine as well – speak to other intentions. Our present situation could drag on for a long time but it would wreck me because I'd always still consider you my wife and don't know what I'd do if I actually ran into you with someone else. Insane jealously. And hopeless misery for letting things fall apart. You and I have made an absolute wreck of our relationship and I don't think you have the slightest desire to pick up the pieces. Maybe, you've learned from it though. I certainly have.

"And then hopefully the wounds will heal because I won't have to deal with you on an emotional level anymore. I don't think you've felt the same way during the past months because you really don't have the same feelings of love that dwelled inside me.

"I'll never be able to get you entirely out of my life because of Britta and Mark. But at least, I hope I can deal with those feelings."

Instead of sticking to a marriage counseling plan, Larry and I date around. I know I lacked common sense. I thought I could get away with stupid, reckless behavior. Of course, not trying to patch up that marriage led to painful consequences. The family is broken and our children had to put up with a lot from their single parents such as living in two homes and meeting all of Mom and Dad's new friends. Not that the kids didn't have structure and supervision. But there were a lot of changes to digest. I always felt Larry also didn't give 100 percent to saving the marriage. But once you let other people into a relationship, you are doomed as a cohesive couple.

I try hard to make marriage at 21 work. I have a copy of Betty Crocker's "Dinner for Two." It has instructions such as 45 minutes before dinner, pare potatoes. I am soon in a groove making French onion soup, using canned beef broth, and chopping up onions and green peppers to make shrimp Creole. Both my mother, Peggy, and mother-in-law, Arline, are superb homemakers. I just don't have a talent to sew my clothes, bake biscuits from scratch and keep the house spic and span like they do. One time when I complain about fixing dinner after working all day, Larry quizzes me with, "How hard can it be?" He then turns out a perfectly fluffy quiche and becomes a gourmet cook from that day forth. Our grown-up kids still look to him to turn out a wicked birthday dinner for them (fettuccine Alfredo – he makes his own pasta, naturally – and flourless chocolate cake with vanilla sauce).

Larry and I beat each other up with not siding together enough. He goes his way and I go mine. We don't have big vocal brawls. No fists or golf clubs hurled at each other. And unlike Linda and Tom, he never slashes me to pieces.

But I sense a breaking point from this marital turmoil. The PGA death would haunt anyone. I wanted a fresh start a few years earlier. But I had a family firmly rooted.

Finally, the toll of ongoing personal discomfort in my marriage following the 57th Championship lead me to leave Ohio in late 1982. Larry had already left Akron. He went to the *Detroit Free Press*, taking our son Mark to live in Grosse Pointe. We had joint custody. I collected no alimony or child support. With my daughter in a brown, un-air conditioned Pinto, I leave everything I know behind. Mark goes with Larry. I am jobless coming to Florida but I push through the pain of an unraveled union with Larry that once mattered.

Before I leave the Buckeye State though, after I am separated for awhile, I meet a man who truly enjoys a good time. I marry Jobie Smith and he comes with me to St. Petersburg where my parents retired. He drives a U-Haul truck with our pitiful possessions.

We settle into a roach-infested apartment. He's unemployed too, leaving a secure Goodyear firefighter job, in hopes of having a career as a photographer. My new beginning only briefly embraces him. But I am forever grateful how Smith always encouraged me to think more creatively about my work. He liked my writing and propelled me in the direction of pushing myself more. We separate soon and divorce a few years later. He doesn't mind; neither do I. He's not a horrible person and I'm not terrible. We just didn't mesh and didn't give ourselves time to figure that out before marrying. Anyway, he takes off back to Akron where he belongs to rejoin his mother and two sons.

Being sucked into an abusive, humiliating relationship is Linda's downfall. She was just a kid when she married, leaving a mother – who doted on her – for a trying life. I can understand marital unions not working out. I'm not a novice Mrs. any longer. But Tom and Linda's life together is a darkness that comes before a lashing storm I fortunately never had to experience.

Linda is mired in Akron with a disturbed guy for a husband; he's gulled by her work for Firestone and that it involves golf, a huge love in his life. His fists have to land somewhere in his delusional state of mind. Why did I have to give her advice like I knew what I was talking about?

My experiences are on a different plane. My gut reaction is if something doesn't work, go a new direction. Linda stays gaga in love and stays around when someone is hurting her. Linda's selections pre-dated publicity and laws about domestic violence that rolled out in the 1980s.

Interestingly, nearby Cleveland is a real frontrunner. Advocates for victims of domestic violence founded The Center for Prevention of Domestic Violence in 1976, a year after Linda's death; Templum, a similar organization, was founded in 1978. The two non-profits merged in 2001, being hailed as pioneers in the nation. Now there's a Domestic Violence Center 24/7 hotline 216-391-HELP.

A shelter home isn't at Linda's disposal. Now there's a whole system in place with judges, prosecutors, friends, family, neighbors all part of preventing and prosecuting domestic violence cases. But should an onlooker intervene? That remains the burning question. In my wildest imagination, I can't see Linda packing a bag to leave Tom.

I made a wrong judgment in my friendship with Linda. I encouraged a very sweet and lovely young woman to go to her death because I wasn't fully aware of the circumstances. I was in the dark about the danger in which she was enveloped. If she had a fear of Tom, why didn't Linda fear for her children also and flee? Rousing his fury by being mouthy ends Linda's future.

Tom's mental illness seemed to reap him loads of help after he killed his wife, the mother of his children. But where was this understanding and action during those dark days of the Akron winter of 1975?

I still have a lump in my throat whenever I think of leaving Akron. It was exciting to move to Florida where I had no past, no history. I felt a sense of possibility that wasn't possible in Akron. And Florida delivered on all I imagined – the warmth, the Gulf of Mexico's expansiveness, the lushness surrounding me. I love to be outdoors and this is possible year-round. Of course, I was a stranger on the sunny beach and dealt with much loneliness the first few years.

I still cherish Kent State for letting me pursue my journalist dream and nearby Akron for wonderful growing up years. In the almost 30 years since I left Tire Town, I have visited many times, usually to see my sister, go to the May 4 anniversary ceremony at the KSU campus or attend a high school class reunion.

I have left the familiar, every day, little things behind such as the look of a blue-collar neighborhood where big saggy houses have creaky floorboards inside and wood painted gray front porches. I like stepping gingerly down steep basement steps to find a bunch of damp junk. I like looking out through windows on landings. And how the houses are so close together you can see your neighbor dunking toast in sunny side eggs.

Now I soak in Akron through older eyes.

To Linda's mother: Dear Genevieve, I write on a note card to mail, "Expect me the week of Oct. 12th, 2008."

But no sooner do I fire off this note then Dale Antram and Emily Petrarca from the PGA Tournament e-mail me. He still doesn't remember Linda at all after looking at the newspaper clipping I mailed him. He says he worked with Carter mostly out of our office on the design of the PGA logo, bag tags and letterhead.

Petrarca writes: "I had a good day yesterday, calling some people I have worked the tournaments with for many years and each was very helpful – but didn't remember the event of Linda's death, at all! It made me feel better that I wasn't the only person who didn't remember. I finally found a couple who have worked for the tournaments for many years and they both remembered the event because they are friends of the people who took the children to foster. The man who remembers is a lawyer and therefore doesn't prefer to have a conversation with you. I think I really didn't have much luck if you look at the information I was able to get. One of the things I learned is that there seemed to be someone who wanted the event kept as quiet as possible."

There is someone wanting to keep this "event" quiet. Hushing up Linda's murder of 30-plus years ago. Odd.

Chapter Eleven
Firestones in Florida

When you reach Baby Boomer twilight years, it's good to mull. And that's what I do before packing for Ohio.

I would say ours was a typical Tire Capital of the World family growing up. My father worked at B.F. Goodrich in the printing department, my uncle sold household appliances at the Goodyear employee store, another aunt and uncle lived in Firestone Park, my brother started out in Goodrich's mailroom and worked his way up to selling tires internationally. I also dabbled in the bouncy ways of this town, which began producing rubber products in the late 1800s.

Little wonder I swear I still have the smell of freshly-minted bias-ply tires in my nose.

When I was a student at Kent State, just out of journalism curiosity and wanting to see my dad, I joined him on the picket line during a 1967 strike. I still remember wearing a purple plum poor boy-style sweater and matching wool slacks. United Rubber Workers President Peter Bommarito shook my hand as my father introduced me to the union honcho who came to rally the tired troops at Goodrich's gate.

Later, I worked in the mailroom at Goodyear one college summer thanks to my best high school friend, Shirley MacIvor (now Wittman), who was a top-notch secretary there. It was a glorious job where I pushed around a cart to hand out the deliveries as I chatted away. Then Shirley and co-workers would take me to lunch at the nearby Brown Derby restaurant where salad, steak which had a plastic hat toothpick inserted, and baked potato reigned supreme.

In the late 1960s and early 1970s when I am a reporter at the *Beacon Journal* and hot on the local fashion beat, I write about Goodyear's final acceptance of female workers wearing pant suits to the job. This is a Tire Town first (no jeans, please).

The mantra when I attended Kenmore High School is to get a factory job and be set for life. But people my age perhaps didn't have a full grasp that all these benefits during the years were negotiated. If one of my high school friends landed that Firestone job, he had good wages and medical care. But he also had to make sacrifices because companies just didn't roll over to worker demands. This often meant a lot of upheaval in family life with all the strikes and feisty contract talks.

Akron, incorporated as a city in 1865, might have remained a small canal town without the likes of Goodyear and Firestone. In 1869, Goodrich is the first rubber company to settle in Akron.

Though he came late to the tire parade in Akron, the story of Harvey Firestone (in his ancestral Germany, it's Feuerstein) holds much romantic appeal.

Near where I grew up, on the Firestone campus by Akron Plant No. 2, there's a lighted bronze statue of him sitting in a chair – like he's bestowing wisdom on our town.

According to a 2006 chatty write-up by historical novelist Daniel Alef, Firestone grew up in small town Columbiana in 1868. After working in Cleveland for his cousin's Columbus Buggy Co., he eventually transferred to Detroit. Fate brought Henry Ford into the store in 1895. He wanted big wheels for his prototype automobile and Firestone was just the salesman to give the customer what he wanted.

In 1904, when Ford was ready to roll with his vehicle, Firestone pitched his product and came away with an order for 2,000 tires at $55 apiece.

This came after Firestone moved to Akron and established his own Firestone Tire & Rubber Co. in 1900 to manufacture carriage tires.

Firestone tires were soon everywhere, even the tires of choice for the first winner of the Indianapolis 500 in 1911.

On a more serene level, my grandparents listened to "The Voice of Firestone" radio program starting in 1928, playing popular tunes.

Culture. Recreation. Housing. Livelihood. In 1938, Harvey Firestone Sr. died at his estate in Miami Beach. The Firestone family continued to dole out their influence in any community where they lived.

And then they got really lucky – a Firestone actually married a Ford in 1947. According to historical research from the Highland Square Neighborhood Association (a community next to Merriman Road), the Ford/Firestone wedding involving grandchildren of Henry Ford and

Harvey Firestone Sr. is between Martha Parke Firestone (Harvey Jr.'s daughter) and Henry Clay Ford (Edsel Ford's son).

On June 21, 1947, it is our city's wedding of the century. All the Grosse Pointers pour into Akron from Michigan, decked out in finery. The society page writers work overtime.

It's a wild coincidence that here I was set to leave Akron in the early 1980s for St. Petersburg – thinking I was putting behind me all things round and rubbery – when a branch of the Firestones had already come to this Gulf of Mexico city.

What happened to the Firestones in St. Petersburg is the non-storybook side of the family.

Time magazine reports on May 16, 1960 that Harvey Samuel Firestone III, 30, heir and only son of Board Chairman Harvey S. Firestone Jr. of the Firestone Tire & Rubber Co., died of a fall (ruled a suicide by a Cuban judge) from the 20th floor of the Havana Hilton Hotel. Having spastic cerebral palsy, *Time* reports Firestone graduated from law school in 1959, planning to practice in St. Petersburg, where he and his wife and daughter made their home.

Why was he in Cuba? The *Highland Square* online newsletter says that the Firestone company had spent $4 million in 1957 on a new tire plant. But newspaper reports say he was there for a brief vacation with his cousin, David Morgan Firestone, and his future law partner, Everett Cushman.

Why were the young Firestones living in St. Petersburg? Because it's beautiful here and I imagine the warm weather was a boost to the young Firestone's health.

Plus, the West Coast of Florida is familiar to the Firestone family. Most everyone knows the story of the Millionaires' Club. Harvey Firestone Sr. and his pals Thomas Alva Edison and Henry Ford, before Edison's death in 1931, hung out at the inventor's Ft. Myers winter home. The trio put time and money into developing a homegrown plant that would yield rubber.

Edison planted hundreds of experimental shrubs and trees in Ft. Myers, just south of where I now live. His second wife Mina exclaims, according to the "People Who Made History" series edited by Carol Cramer: "Everything has turned to rubber in our family. We talk rubber, think rubber, dream rubber."

I can relate to that, Mina.

Down the line, Firestone III is probably comfortable with St. Petersburg due to these family vacations and visits. He chooses to get his law degree at St. Petersburg's Stetson Law School. He marries an Ohio schoolteacher, Beverly Lou McFarlan, in 1956 and the young couple, according to *St. Petersburg Times* archives, move into a seven-room house made of Tennessee granite in our sunshine city.

The newspaper makes light of this, probably because Firestone's boyhood home back in Akron at 50 Twin Oaks, next to Portage Country Club, is a 1926-built French chateau style with eight bedrooms and bathrooms on 1.66 acres. (While this house still stands, it's sad that Harbel Manor, across the street where Harvey Firestone Sr. lived, has only a historic wall remaining of that compound.) In addition, the Firestones had a massive spread at Ocean Lawn in tony Newport, R.I.

The Firestone daughter from this brief union is Diane Elizabeth, born Sept. 15, 1958. Her name is now listed as a benefactor for at least two St. Petersburg institutions, Shorecrest Preparatory School and Eckerd Youth Ranch.

Mary Evertz, who was the *Times'* longtime social writer, has a vivid memory of the Firestone clan in St. Petersburg. While Harvey Firestone III was still a student at Stetson, she covered the dedication of the Firestone apartments (dorms) on campus. She recalls hearing about the fraternity parties Firestone would host at his house, off Park Street on the south side. "Firestone was well-liked," says Evertz. "He overcame great physical difficulty to get through law school. His fraternity brothers used to tie drumsticks to his hands so he could be part of their band at parties. He flailed around a lot but he never hesitated to join in."

Evertz says at the time after his death in Cuba, it was suspected that the son of an American millionaire industrialist met foul play. "I mean how could he pull himself up to a window and jump out?" she asks of the wheelchair-bound Firestone.

Firestone's family told the media at the time he could stand and walk. They reasoned his death was accidental – the young Firestone toppled over the terrace while looking out. His cousin David Morgan Firestone told law enforcement authorities, according to the *Miami News*, though, that Harvey III tried to jump out of a moving car two months earlier. So the Cuba authorities did rule suicide.

When asked about an official Firestone stance today, Bridgestone Americas' spokeswoman Elizabeth Lewis e-mails me from Nashville, Tenn.: "For Harvey Firestone (III), unfortunately, I do not know anything further." A corporate memory does not go back 50 years, for sure.

The Firestone cousin subsequently dropped the "David" from his name and Morgan Firestone moved to Canada in 1968 to head Firestone Canada. He became a Canadian citizen, was known for his love of horse racing and charity work and died in January 2009 after suffering from a neurodegenerative illness similar to Parkinson's disease, according to *The Hamilton Spectator*. Cushman, the other person on the Cuba trip, died in the early 1980s – he was much older than the Firestone heir and served as his tutor.

Evertz knew his widow when Beverly Lou Firestone married a St. Petersburg physician Paul Wallace. They had a daughter, Nancy, who attended Canterbury School of Florida, a private school, with Evertz's daughter Wendy.

Evertz explains that Beverly Lou and Paul Wallace were eventually divorced. "They had a nice boat. We used to go out with them in Placido Bayou," she recalls of happier times. Beverly Lou Firestone Wallace moved away. But the Firestone name lingers in St. Petersburg.

Firestone Jr. gave the commencement address at his son's graduation from Stetson in 1959, the year before the 30-year-old son allegedly killed himself. (Harvey III had three sisters, including the one who marries the Ford.)

Stetson Law's Great Hall still has a touch of Firestone in one of its historic rooms where there's a fireplace plus arched alcoves. For this former dining room, Harvey

Firestone Jr. donates Flemish tapestry, believed to be woven in the latter part of the 17th century. The Great Hall hosts a lot of legal lectures and events at Stetson, Florida's first law school.

Stetson spokesperson Brandice Palmer says the law school also has a Firestone suite. "It's very nice, not like a dorm room. It's where special guests stay when they visit," she says.

One cool morning I meet Michael Swygert, professor of law emeritus at Stetson. He has written a massive 746-page book on the history of the law school and, of course, has devoted a few pages to Firestone III.

Walking around the Mediterranean Revival designed campus, a former 1920s hotel, with its pinkish/orange buildings, Swygert first shows me the tapestries. There are two, one about 10 feet by 4 feet picturing a fancy hunting scene. This has hung in Mann Hall since 1961. There's another tapestry about as large as a two king size quilts with birds, ships and trees in the Great Hall which used to be the dining room for the hotel.

There are no signs regarding the Firestone donation. Swygert is baffled by this lack of recognition but he quickly leads me to a swimming pool complex. Here Firestone III is honored. The recreation center is named after him. Unfortunately, Firestone Jr., who contributed $150,000 in early 1973 for the project, dies that June, one year before the complex is finished.

In 1974 during the opening ceremonies, Firestone III's daughter Diane attends and sees the large granite stone (still there) which reads:

Stetson University College of Law
Recreation Center in Memory of Harvey Firestone III
1930-1960
Graduated L.L.B., Class of 1959
Admitted to the Florida Bar, 1960

White-haired Swygert, 70, who looks sporty in a black jacket, is quite the researcher who knows on what page items are contained in his weighty book without looking at the index. He uncovered what brought the young Firestone to Florida – a link between Akron and St. Petersburg that is set forever.

In 1954, Harvey Firestone Jr. wrote a letter, available in Stetson's archives, to then-Florida Governor Doyle Carlton asking which law school would be best suited for his son, who had been largely home schooled before earning a degree at the University of Miami. Carlton suggested Stetson. The school has many ground floor classrooms and offices as it's built in a courtyard layout. So Firestone III is among the first students at Stetson in Gulfport after the law school relocates from Deland on the East Coast.

Swygert, who lost his own brother when his sibling was 14, says a parent never gets over the death of a child. He expresses sadness about the loss in the Firestone family, showing how intimate a researcher of his caliber becomes with his subjects. And he also says he feels sorry that Firestone III never learned he had passed the bar. This news came weeks after his death.

"He couldn't write but he got special permission to take the bar by reading each question. Harvey would then dictate his answers to an assistant dean at Stetson. A standard blue book is used," explains Swygert. Firestone III's name remains anonymous during the test grading as is the practice.

As near as Swygert can calculate, the Firestone family contributed more than $200,000 to Stetson, which in today's money could be close to a million. "I believe the tapestries are probably worth more now than the pool," says Swygert.

Former Stetson Dean Bruce Jacob was a classmate of Firestone III's and has vivid memories of how the young man struggled with his physical limitations. Jacob calls me as I'm taking my granddaughters to ballet so after I park them in class, I go to my vehicle and return his call. When Jacob was dean, he had the tapestries appraised. "It was about $8,000 25 years ago," he says.

"Harvey was a wonderful guy. He could hardly talk but he tried. What it took the average person three to four minutes to say, it took him 15 minutes," says Jacob.

Firestone was wheeled around campus and lived in an apartment now called the Firestone Suite. Jacob says even after he married, Firestone spent a good deal of time in his campus abode, the layout made accessible for his wheelchair. This is customary for law students to remain on campus because they have to cram 24/7 all that detailed case information.

Jacob remembers an annual Christmas event Firestone sponsored where community children who had mental and physical challenges came to campus for cookies and entertainment.

He doesn't buy the suicide theory. "Anyone who knew him would never believe it. His legs were spindly.

He could never have gotten out that window unless it was an accident where he toppled over," says Jacob.

Jacob learned the news after leaving law school to serve in the Army. "I heard about it right away. His death stunned everyone. Everybody liked him. Harvey was very intelligent and a great guy."

In her masters' thesis a few years ago, Lois Orr, then a University of Akron student, ponders how attached Harvey's mother, Elizabeth, was to her handicapped son. "His health and welfare were Elizabeth's responsibilities," she writes. Reached in Akron, Orr says she enjoyed the research on Elizabeth Parke Firestone, whose legacy is a donation of a vast collection of couture clothes. These went to UA in 1989 and 1991. "Akron has so many fascinating women who never gained much in the way of recognition," Orr says.

Orr found a quaint, casual 1939 family portrait of the Firestones when Harvey III is about nine years old to include in her thesis. Elizabeth is almost cuddling the boy who wears braces around his shoes. The picture is from the Benson Ford Research Center in Dearborn, Mich.

Orr also interviews Charles Billow, a longtime funeral home director in Akron, and he recalls many times transporting the young Firestone to the hospital via his company's ambulance service when the boy had health problems. Billows also notes to Orr that neither the *Beacon Journal* nor the *New York Times* ran obituaries of Harvey Samuel Firestone III's death. The family simply declined this service.

The death of Harvey Firestone III is a great loss. Who wouldn't admire his grit as he starts a young family and finishes at Stetson. Floridians may only vaguely know this connection between Firestone and St. Petersburg. But this is the kind of knowledge Akronites eat for lunch.

As for Harvey's daughter, Firestone family spokesman Bob Troyer, who graduated with me from Kent State in 1968, says he hasn't heard from or seen Diane Firestone in years. "I know at one time she was living in Costa Rica," he says from his Chicago office.

I tell him to look on the Internet. She's pictured there as a pretty blonde. In 2005, the now 51-year-old Diane, Harvey Firestone III's only child, donated her cattle ranch in Costa Rica to Pitzer College in California. I tell him the college's public relations woman Anna Chang isn't very forthcoming, only to say Diane is part of the Firestone tire family.

"The Firestones are very private people," says Troyer.

"But what about Andrew?" I ask, referring to the reality TV star featured once on "The Bachelor."

"Andrew broke rank," says Troyer.

So Harvey Firestone III's death shall remain somewhat a mystery.

Firestone lore, including weddings and funerals, prevailed over Akron day and night. It seems even for the enchanted, there can be moments of fury followed by heartbreak. This isn't easily dismissed in anyone's life, even millionaires.

Chapter Twelve
Praying Hands for a Life Cut Short

Fall in Ohio attaches itself to all your senses. I'm glad to be back in autumn 2008.

My first stop is Firestone Metro Park, a neighbor of the Firestone Country Club. This park is not only colorful but smells fresh and woodsy.

The club itself looks like a large Brady family-style home, set on vivid green grass visually stunning against the changing leaves.

The park area used to be a dairy farm. But in 1949 Firestone Tire and Rubber Co. donated the land to the city. The 89 acres were gradually built up with more property additions and now stands at 258 acres.

There are wetland, meadow and forest areas and as a young family, we went to this park constantly. So it was a good start to my Ohio trip to visit here.

Now the recreation building is gone and instead there's an open air shelter. But I see across the field that the picnic tables to which we used to lug all our gear remain where flat land transforms to thick woods.

The hill where we took our sled in the winter remains but it looks not so menacing now. I guess I'm having the typical "everything looks grand in size when you're a kid" reaction.

Next on the agenda is Rose Hill Burial Park. This is such a beautiful cemetery, you could pack a picnic and stay awhile. I choose to have lunch at the nearby Summit Mall with my friend from high school Shirley Wittman, the sparkling woman who once got me the Goodyear job.

Since it's crunchy leaf time in Ohio, I'm telling Shirley about my sister's neighbor who has trees full of Northern Spy apples, made known by Johnny Appleseed. That's a satisfying Midwest experience to pluck a crisp apple off a backyard tree and chomp down.

But our mission is to look up Linda's grave. Shirley's a good sport. But then she's known me for almost 50 years. She waits in the car while I go next door to Bokas Funeral Home for instructions on how to find the marker. Rose Hill cemetery is 120 acres!

I have to chuckle when the man inside informs me that famous people such as Rex Humbard and Dallas Billington are buried at Rose Hill. Maybe only an Akronite would be impressed by this. These were two TV evangelists who had enormous congregations in Tire Town. I once had a freelance writing job at The Chapel in University Park which back in the 1970s had almost 5,000 members. Big churches do well in Akron.

Shirley and I walk in the direction on the print-out map. Linda's grave is close to the West Market Street and Smith Road intersection, a major thoroughfare.

She's in spot 68, near the storage building. A caretaker walks us right up to the grave. There are praying hands on the tiny marker. Linda M. McLain, May 16, 1947 to February 5, 1975. It reads "daughter" on the flat brass plate.

"She was killed by her husband," I announce to the Rose Hill caretaker who shakes his head. He seems very sympathetic even though I'm sure his days consist of sad tales.

It's one thing to see the grave of an older person, especially one who is racked by pain in later years. It's another experience to see where young, pretty Linda is in the cold ground. I wish I had brought flowers. I lean down and put my hand on the marker as if to make a connection. This plain marker is all that reminds the world that Linda once lived. She was much more vibrant than this patch of earth.

I'd like to see the house where the McLain children grew up after their mother is murdered. It's in Fairlawn, a higher end suburb of Akron not far from Rose Hill. James and Eva Miller lived in what looks like a comfy family home, a large, white brick Colonial with black shutters. The back of the house appears to be an add-on.

Next we go across town to where Linda and Tom lived which turns out to be very close to Linda's mother, Genevieve Miller.

Shirley points out a giant bare lot as she drives through an industrial section of Akron. It is where General Tire used to stand. This factory isn't shuttered; it's gone! The site was cleared of the huge factory about the year 2000.

A bulldozed factory is not a pretty sight. The McLains, of course, lived near General Tire in East Akron when all things were humming inside.

The young couple resided a few streets over where there are tiny houses, some in disarray, most tidy. Their address no longer exists. Instead there is an apartment complex, built in a small valley.

The Sanginiti house where Tom killed himself is not too far away but in a better community called Ellet. It's a one story with a pit bull warning door sign. I guess I'm surprised the house is so modest because Sanginitis with its salmon-colored interior and cloth napkins was a classy restaurant in its heyday.

As we drive to Genevieve's, I'm shocked this residence of death is so near to her. I've been to her house before but this is new to me to realize she is in the same neighborhood where the Sanginitis once lived and where Tom killed himself.

Genevieve's street is still working class but definitely a nicer area, away from the shadow of the defunct factory complex.

She greets us in a housecoat; comfortable after a morning of getting her curly dark hair fixed at the beauty parlor. She puts her feet up in a recliner and I notice her living room has new drapes and carpet.

She and Shirley hit it off with their shared experiences of being rubber city secretaries. Genevieve says she used to walk to work at General, even in freezing cold weather.

They both don't like the catty atmosphere of women working together where one lady is boss (or thinks she is). Genevieve sounds like she had true gumption raising Linda and keeping her outgoing personality in check to work in such a structured place.

She tells me again of meeting her third husband and has a formal portrait of them resting on her TV stand.

She almost talks herself into once again volunteering in a nursing home. This was volunteer work she and her late husband did.

But she reminds herself she's pretty content with this new life. She loves to go to restaurants and has relatives from her last marriage nearby to hang out with.

We don't talk of Linda's death too much. Unlike our first meeting, she's no longer raw over her daughter's death. Why rehash everything we have spent years talking about? Instead of hand wringing, Genevieve is enjoying the moment.

Before we leave, she stops me in the driveway to give advice. "Live it up, kiddo," she says with a knowing smile.

That weekend, my son, Mark, drives down from his Grosse Pointe Farms, Mich., home with my grandson, Jack, now 10, to attend the Kent State homecoming. It's good for Mark to leave behind the turmoil of the automobile industry and it's good for me to hang out with Jack, who eagerly accepts my gift of a Kent State T-shirt from a campus store.

We watch a very homespun parade down Main Street and then sip coffee with KSU journalism alumni and instructors. Later, as we walk around town before lunching at Ray's, the bar of distinction in Kent, my son asks me earnestly, "Why did we ever leave here?"

There isn't time to go into that.

Chapter Thirteen
Present Day Reporting

Because of my mother's extended illness and then death in April 2009, I am in a state of melancholy. It's the lowest depth of human misery to watch a loved one suffer through an illness – in her case, crippling pain trying to be mobile, the aftermath somewhat of her teenage polio. When she dies, it's not a relief to me although I'm glad she won't have to scrunch up her face anymore when trying to lift out of a chair. I miss her voice on the phone terribly.

To get my mind off dying and death, I babysit my granddaughters, Clare and Halle, and have a good time watching them grow. But their friction as two sisters reminds me of my own sibling rivalry with my younger sister. I wasn't too nice. Growing up, my sister is short and blonde and I am taller and brunette. Our physical looks aren't the only things worlds apart. We never seem to agree.

The same for my granddaughters, Halle and Clare. So when I hear Halle say childish, mean things to younger Clare, I cringe.

Just a few years ago, I found a senior graduation photo of my sister. On the back in 1968, she wrote,

"Dear John (she always called me that because I was a tree-climbing tomboy and she was a little kewpie doll growing up),

"A very nice person to have for a sister, but I wouldn't want you around all the time. Please try to treat me a little nicer. Cool it with the Mrs. Miller impressions (a former neighbor who had a squeaky voice) and the articles (ouch, she didn't like my writing).

Your loving sister

I must say I really bonded with my brother and sister as our parents lapse into terrible declines. Why couldn't we all have gotten along growing up? I used to tease my younger sister and tried to punch the heck out of my older brother.

But believe me, we are all bawling our eyes out together – let bygones be bygones, well almost – when our beloved parents pass.

Getting my emotions in control takes awhile after sweet Peg's death. I don't continue recounting this PGA tragedy until the fall of 2009 because of the stress of losing my mom.

I am now without living parents. My dad Pete dies in 2004. No matter how ill they were – and old age really knocked the stuffing out of my parents – it's still painful to be without people who loved me so dearly.

My older brother lives in Greenville, S.C., after being transferred there by Michelin which had bought out Goodrich. He and his wife were the chief caretakers for my ailing parents who had moved there from Florida as their health began to fall apart. My sister in Ohio and I in Florida had long distance worries. But we spend the fall of 2008 to spring 2009, making lots of trips to Greenville.

I know I am fortunate to have had Pete and Peggy in my life so long. They were both in their 80s when they die. Their graveside services, held in Akron, made me feel good they were back home together.

My father was of sturdy Romanian stock. It's amazing he didn't speak English when arriving for the first day of kindergarten because he is born in the United States. Later, he is known for his beautiful penmanship and expressive letters.

My mother, who grew up in nearby Hudson, is equally hard-working. Despite that bout of polio, which shriveled her left leg, she graduates with her class at age 18 from Hudson High School. She'd always admonish me to "stand up, straight as a board." I can hardly call this posture advice "nagging," because she had curvature of the spine.

They surprised everyone by leaving Ohio in the early 1980s to move to sunny Florida. When my dad retires at age 60 from Goodrich, he announces he didn't want to shovel snow and deal with the hill where we lived in Kenmore, a cohesive community next to Akron's downtown, on icy days. I follow them as soon as I could with my dad's encouragement, "Tampa Bay has two newspapers – one of them will hire you!"

I didn't have a "poor me" childhood. Despite the smelly tire dump across the street over our back fence causing black grime on our windowsills, we enjoyed our back yard. The huge Firestone factory headquarters is easily within walking distance but we learn to live with this industrial neighbor.

In our urban paradise, we have trees to scamper up, a grape arbor swing and a wonderful hill for our sleds.

My grandfather plants a large garden on his one-acre property. With a contingent of aunts, uncles and cousins, we all live (or rather squeeze) into his apartment building. In our second floor unit, my parents sleep on a pull-out sofa bed while my sister and I share one room and my brother takes the other.

The tire dump locale isn't ideal for any one's health, I learn recently. My St. Petersburg physician sends me a radiology report. It states there is evidence of old granulomatous disease on my lungs. My doctor writes on the report: "Old exposure to what? Where were you raised?"

Yet slight lung damage or not, I had a touch of glamour in my life. I wasn't 100 percent tomboy. I did live outdoors though when the weather was mild, playing from early morning to when the street lights came out without any "helicopter" adults telling me what to do.

For years in grade school, my mother diligently drives me to tap dance lessons at the downtown studio of Johnnie and Dona Del Dixon. I perform in several of their dance reviews and think I am very special, even coming up with the stage name "Noel Hedge."

All this urban grit mixed with tap dancing in neighborhood driveways ended right before I entered sixth grade. Our brick apartment building is hit by a wrecker's ball to make way for an interstate ramp. We move from 4th Street to 21st Street in Kenmore.

It was at this new school that my sixth grade teacher, Norris Mooney, thought I should be a journalist because I like to write essays. So my tap dancing dream for the future went out the window.

Speaking of my bedroom window, one morning on 21st Street I watch the *Beacon Journal's* top reporter Helen Waterhouse bang on the side door across the street. She is looking to interview a neighbor, a traveling business man, trapped in Cuba when the island is taken over by Castro. He is newly released from the troubled island and sent home. And there is industrious Waterhouse ready to go for the kill, er the interview. That kind of gumption, along with a headful of Brenda Starr comics, seal my wanting to be a journalist.

Akron has changed since my last few years there in the early 1980s and then it hasn't. But an update is in order.

Firestone has hosted the World Golf Championships-Bridgestone Invitational since 2006. The agreement with Bridgestone has been extended until 2014. There are about 75 players, half of what the PGA tournament attracts but there are no cuts at Firestone.

Receptionist Glenda Buchanan says their office space is now on the golf site, not downtown. "It's much better than moving from downtown at the last minute," she says. The space is at the opposite end of the country club property where a media room can handle upwards of 120 sports writers although the number sometimes grew to over 300 media types when Tiger Woods was in town. No more hot-as-blazes tents for scribes.

The tournament, planned for Aug. 3-8 in 2010, has 1,000 volunteers who wear khaki slacks and polo shirts. The website asks for $75 from volunteers for their meals, credentials, volunteer party and uniforms, informing that women may also wear skirts, capris or knee-length shorts. Women get a choice of visor or cap but men have to wear the logo caps. An optional item is a Rabbit Island hat; it keeps the sun off. Volunteers also get jackets. So everything is a lot more casual than the 1975 prim dress.

Tickets are sold via Ticketmaster. I'm sure no one misses the Izod sheaths. But those Ticketmaster fees!

The volunteer party is slated for Aug. 1, 2010. I wonder where my sequin butterfly dress is.

One of the volunteers I'm able to reach on the telephone, e-mails me an impressive bit of volunteer history.

Akron optometrist Larry Barger, 66, who I remember as having a Lancelot hair cut and rimless glasses back when he was 32 in 1975, says there's little chance to watch golf when you are a volunteer. His job was to escort players through the throngs of fans trying to get autographs. If a golfer wanted law enforcement security back then, Barger and the Security and Safety committee would set it up. He writes: "In 1975, this was my sixth year of involvement on the tournament committee and I was on the Security and Safety committee, chaired by Dave Franklin.

"Franklin died very early in life due to cancer, and the Dave Franklin Award was created in his honor for the volunteer who exemplified what Dave stood for, the 'model volunteer.' This award has grown in stature and is the highest honor that is bestowed each year to a worthy volunteer. One of my fondest memories was learning the 'ropes' by following Dave Franklin. His legacy will continue as long as there is professional golf at Firestone Country Club.

"As I look over the committee structure 35 years ago, many have moved away, many have died but 20 of us who were on the tournament committee then still continue to volunteer. Eleven of us have become the chairman of events that followed the 57th PGA. I was chairman of the 1990 NEC World Series of Golf. This past tournament was my 41st year of volunteering. We honored five who have been involved for over 50 years, including the 57th PGA.

"As I look at the pictures of us 35 years ago, the tournament has grown, we have gotten older. As I look at those of us who still volunteer, we were part of the family that put on the 57th PGA and we continue to be a part of the family of volunteers that are helping to put on the best show in golf in Akron each year. Simply put, it's in our blood."

Bernie Antonino, who retired as a schoolteacher in 2000 and has been a Firestone golf volunteer for 43 years, would agree.

"I'll keep doing it as long as it's fun," she says from her Wadsworth home.

Antonino doesn't remember Linda's death. "Unfortunately or maybe fortunately, I do not," she says.

Because of her ties to Firestone (she often volunteers in the Bridgestone office), she's made some lasting friends, including Jack and Barbara Nicklaus.

"I don't know how it happened. Just years ago when everyone was paying attention to Jack, I struck up a conversation with Barbara. Then I was bringing them my pizzelles (Italian cookies). They send me a Christmas card and tickets to Jack's Memorial tournament in Dublin, Ohio every year."

Raymond Sanginiti, the brother of the late Dominic who was Tom McLain's stepfather, answers the phone on a sunny September morning. He says the restaurant closed in 1989 and he's delighted to hear that menus sell on e-Bay and postcards of the E. Market Street place are online for viewing. In the early 2000s, he sold the property to Haven of Rest, a homeless shelter.

He denies a connection of his brother whose wife, Pat, was Tom's mother, to the 1975 killing. "There was no murder in our family," he says, after I lay out a few details.

I know I have the right Sanginiti as Dominic's 1985 obituary states he was a partner and the treasurer of the restaurant.

Richard Guster, who chaired the PGA event, has a fresher memory. He remembers well the 57th PGA tournament and verbally goes play-by-play of Nicklaus' win. He recalls how the great golfer got out of what was considered an unplayable shot on the 625 yards of the 16th hole. The big lake is a huge challenge, Guster adds. But Nicklaus swung hard to get over the tree, avoiding also what was then a route for power lines.

"Nicklaus used a 9 iron to get on the green and putted it in to insure his victory," he says, adding the day ended brilliantly. "It was something considering he started with a lousy tee shot."

Guster recalls how Nicklaus has often said (and written in "My Story") that the shot remains his biggest gamble in a major.

Guster and his wife, Sharlee, are friends with Nicklaus and his wife, Barbara, and also were "good friends" with J. Edwin Carter and his wife, M.J. "They were our way in to the Masters each year," he said, of the Carter couple obtaining hard-to-get tickets for them for Augusta.

He says Carter orchestrated all three PGA Championships in Akron, 1960, 1966 and 1975. He also was the impetus in Akron hosting the World Series of Golf.

Guster says Carter died in about 1997 and his wife, M.J., in 2004. That would make Carter about 91 years old at his death; he is 69 in 1975.

I've been no fan of musty Carter's, but I am bewildered that the PGA doesn't recognize his contribution. I have sent e-mails to different branches of the golf organization and placed phone calls and no one seems to remember the guy. I e-mail the World Golf Hall of Fame in St. Augustine, Fla., and its curator Mark Cubbedge writes back: "I do not have anything on Mr. Carter and our limited archives deal primarily with Hall of Fame members. We had a massive exhibition on Nicklaus a few years ago as part of our rotating exhibition program, but we have since replaced that with an exhibition on Bob Hope. So I'm afraid what we had on that event is no longer viewable."

Guster just went to the funeral for M.G. O'Neil, whose family founded O'Neil's Department Store and was the CEO of General Tire. O'Neil also served on the board for the 57th Tournament. He later received national attention when his stepdaughter Patricia Bowman is the accuser in the Kennedy rape trial in West Palm Beach.

"That seems to be what life is about now – going to funerals," Guster says.

Guster, retired as an attorney in 1994, says he fell off the golf volunteer bandwagon after Akron no longer hosted PGA tournaments. But his wife just received a 50-year award for her efforts.

When I tell him how Carter fretted that Akron wouldn't come through with money for the 57th PGA, Guster says firmly the 1975 tournament was successful financially and gave one-third of its revenues to Akron Children's Hospital.

In fact, the Akron tournaments have been a boon for the city's non-profits and other charitable organizations. In the 1975 PGA program, Don Padgett, PGA Secretary (his grandson now runs the Bridgestone Invitational at Firestone), writes: "And a whole parade of Rubber City Opens, American Golf Classics, PGA Championships and World Series of Golf has poured nearly a million dollars into the pet local projects of the Akron Jaycees, Kiwanis Club, the *Beacon Journal* Charity Fund and the Women's Board of the Children's Hospital of Akron."

Bridgestone now counts that number at about $18 million going to charity through the ages with $918,1000 raised by the 2009 Bridgestone Invitational.

Guster, who I remember as lanky with deep-set dark circles around his blue eyes, laughs when I tell him I still have a copy of the tournament souvenir book. "The cover was yellow and then there was that drawing of Simon Perkins," he says, chuckling. Yes, the yellow is an icky mustard color. And Perkins, an early settler of Northeast Ohio who surveyed the city in 1825, is sketched to look more like chubby Santa Claus.

Guster recalls Linda's death. "It was an awful, awful tragedy," he says. "I've lost track of the children involved but I knew James Miller as a grand guy. He and Eva were wonderful to those children."

Guster adds, "I know in that situation back then, there wasn't much protection for a woman. Today, there is. But domestic violence still happens everywhere. It's just a terrible thing."

The next day I open the *St. Petersburg Times* to a front-page story about a boyfriend murdering the mother of his twins. A judge had earlier dismissed the dead woman's temporary injunction against her killer because she didn't show up in court. She told relatives, "That's my babies' daddy."

Chapter Fourteen
Knowing Linda

I reach Jody McLain, Linda's oldest daughter, at her work as a social worker. I let her know right off that I'm working on a story about the 1970s period in my life, focusing on Linda's death. She promises to call me when she gets home and does. She has Linda's wonderful voice.

She's glad I called because she says she has limited knowledge of what happened in her childhood. "I have so many emotions. I grew up with that void of not having parents," she says.

Jody, 42, says she wants desperately for the pieces to fit together. She believes it will be good to talk with me because I can be objective and not hold the biases that exist in her family.

I fill her in as best I can, even telling her about that fatal day when I told Linda she needed to speak up to Tom. I tell her about Tom taking Linda to lunch and her returning awfully upset.

"What happened at lunch?" she asks.

I can only speculate, I explain, that either Tom is highly agitated again about the job situation or he threatened Linda. But I add, he does go home with

Kara and life in the family seemed normal routine that evening. Then the murder.

"We were there," she says quietly of that fatal night. "When you're an adult those memories stick in your head."

Before Tom passes away, she receives letters from him and has visitations but never in connection with the Millers. She went to Grandma Pat's (Sanginiti) house where she and her brother and sister would go out to dinner with their dad when he was on one of his passes from the mental institution.

She never asked him directly about the murder. "I was mature for my age so I did notice how fragile he was emotionally. But we never sat and talked," she says. On all these visits, Tom didn't appear to be drugged up to her.

"I have a lot more memories of my dad than I do of my mom, " she says flatly, adding that she was six when her mom died and 12 when Tom committed suicide.

In her possession is her baby book but she says Grandma Genevieve because of her hatred of Tom hasn't been as forthcoming as Jody hoped she would be through the years. "I can understand. She's never been right since losing her daughter," she concludes.

Jody first attended Ohio State and then became pregnant at the end of her first year. Raised by a single mom, her son, Sebastian Hopson, 22, has an achieving mom. Jody recently earned her master's degree.

She repeats many times during our talk, "It has a big affect on your life when you grow up without your parents." The Millers gave her everything materially but she recalls growing up in their home as not easy because they were emotionally distant.

Then too, she had a confusing mix of tragedy and privilege. "It was a strange situation. They hadn't been a big part of my life before I lost my mom. So it was a difficult adjustment. It was like living with someone you don't know." She says she and her mom rarely went to the Millers' home in Fairlawn.

Since Kara was two years old when Linda was killed, she says it was easier for her to adapt. And then there's Jody's son, who she says is bonded to the Millers. She says he was devastated when Jim Miller died as he grew up close to the couple who took in the McLain children.

"I was attached to my parents. You love your parents no matter what happens," she says.

Yet she doesn't believe the Millers fully understood her loyalty to her father. "They had anger toward my one parent. So it was awkward and painful to be in their home. I kept wishing they would stop bashing my dad."

Jody says there's never been an open dialogue in her family about Linda's death. Her brother Scott told her son without her permission and she admits she's a bit surprised that her son has never asked for more details.

Jody went to Central-Hower High School in the city and Scott and Kara to Firestone High School in Fairlawn. Jody wanted to get into social services, feeling her life experiences would give her more understanding of what stress and strain can do to some lives.

"The Millers were very stoic. They were nurturing in that they would provide us with every opportunity we would have never had otherwise. But there was no objectivity when they did talk about things," she says. I say the World War II generation tend to keep things close to their vest and not reveal too much personal. She says that could partly be the reason for the hush-up. Then too, the Millers were part of Akron Old Guard, where the Portage Country Club lifestyle meant keeping up respectability, I say. Yes, that sounds right, says Jody.

Jody says she was awake when Tom murdered Linda. "I was old enough to know something bad happened but not old enough to know why," she says.

She says her dad knew what he did was wrong immediately and called 911. "He was horribly distraught," she says.

She's cautious about telling friends and co-workers about her past. "I don't want them to judge. People have struggles, they snap. We aren't talking about my dad being evil here."

Tom suffered from depression and anxiety and demons "we will never understand," says Jody, who adds her life has been a long road. Now Linda has three grandchildren and Jody faces middle age feeling lonely without that comforting presence of her mom.

Her favorite memory is what she calls Payday Fridays. Linda would buy her an Avon critter pin with a hidden container of solid perfume when our PGA work money came through.

"I just don't hear that kind of stuff," she says, when I compare her soothing voice to her mother's. "When you asked if I was Linda's daughter earlier on the phone, I broke down and cried when I thought about it later. I just don't hear that kind of stuff," she repeats.

I tell her to have Scott and Kara call me. She promises to ask them. But I know either I'll hear from them right away or not at all. I hear nothing from Linda's other kids.

It happens in every family to run from some difficult stuff going on at home. But dad killing mom is beyond comprehension. If support isn't there to face the truth or at least vent your frustrations, then it would indeed cause a lot of confusion and ill feelings.

I can't imagine what Jody and her siblings deep-down feelings are like but it sounds as if fearlessness with the facts isn't a part of the mix of their interaction, even today. But who am I to judge?

I guess Scott and Kara don't want to hear what I have to say because churning up damaging memories isn't pleasant. I can only imagine their misgivings about reaching out to me.

But I had to at least reach Scott. He turns out to be friendly and open over the phone, just like his mother. He says he thought of writing a book himself about the tragedy of his parents but his fitness work keeps him busy.

He says in years past, he told people his parents died in an accident. "I know that sounds creepy saying that," he says. "But it's a complicated story."

Scott says his life went from being on the free lunch program for impoverished families at elementary school to leisurely brunch at Portage Country Club after church.

Scott says his family lived in Florida before moving back to Ohio in the summer of 1974. His early childhood consisted of a lot of moving around – he would change schools constantly.

"I know as horrible as this sounds but I wonder if I would have ever gone to college if my life had stayed the same with my parents," he says. "Good or bad – we lived a rough life. I can remember my mom making us tomato soup out of ketchup and water."

Scott says his unstable, blue-collar family life involved mental illness and yes, domestic violence. "I remember my dad being treated in the past for his problems. And I witnessed him beating my mom several times."

Scott says he's tried to piece together "How did this all go down" on his own. He's best friends with (since the fifth grade) Kelly Clark, the son of the late Ron Clark who was a top editor at the *Akron Beacon Journal.*

"It is so important for me to have a lifelong friend after all the upheaval in my life," he says. Plus, the Clarks helped him find newspaper articles about the murder of his mother. "Today it would be on 24-hour news," he says. "But it takes a little digging to find this case."

Scott was 13 when his dad died. He calls his memories of their conversations "strong."

"My dad explained what happened. He said he and my mom got into a heated argument. He thought she was sleeping with some other guy. But I realized that was just his paranoia talking. He starting stabbing her after she said she was leaving him and taking the kids. He told me the experience was like looking through a tunnel – like an out-of-body experience. "

Scott doesn't sound emotional like Jody when discussing this tragedy.

He says his dad did well on lithium after the murder. "It calmed him down. Before he was either on top of the world – all pumped up. Or the lowest of low."

As for how his world was after losing his mother, Scott says there were lots of conflicts with all the relatives. "We kids loved both our parents but our aunt and uncle had a lot of hate toward my dad. I think they felt guilty too that they didn't step in beforehand and do something."

Scott remembers his mom as smart. "One day she said, 'We vote for McGovern because we're poor. Uncle Jimmy votes for Nixon because he's rich.'" As a bright child, Scott says he made mental notes of the route the funeral procession took from the Akron funeral home to the Fairlawn grave. "I don't know why I remember directions like that," he says chuckling.

Scott says today when he's working with clients hoping to lose weight and get in shape, he notices the birthdate - if it's his mom's year (1947) or his dad's (1941).

"I think about them all the time. But you know, that wasn't the most traumatic thing in my life," he says, his voice getting considerably lower in volume. "It was my divorce. That may sound horrible but kids are kind of resilient. I was married from 1995 to 2004 and when that was over, it hurt like nothing else had."

Scott is also introspective about his family. "I wonder with all my dad's problems if the apple doesn't fall far from the tree. There are times when I really wonder what life is all about. I get down but I have to say with pride I don't stay down."

Scott says he doesn't get to Akron much. But he expresses affection for Linda's mother, his grandmother Gen.

"I loved my father deeply so that causes problems with my grandma. But I would never condone what my dad did. I lived it. I know how wrong it was," he says, sounding as if he's ready to conclude our conversation.

But then I ask him about his dad's state-of-mind before his death in 1980.

Scott says he visited Tom at Massillon State Hospital. "There were people there who were rocking back and forth and drooling. They were profoundly mentally ill. And my dad would be sitting there reading a newspaper. He had normal intelligence. We could talk golf and politics. He expressed a great fear of going to prison."

But Scott says he did see an incident where it showed him how ill his dad was. They stopped at a roadside restroom one day returning from Massillon to Akron and Tom came running out and dove into the car. "He said that someone had stuffed toilet paper rolls in the toilets and that reminded him of what patients often did at Massillon. So he thought 'they' were out to get him there."

Scott says Tom's mother, Pat Sanginiti, didn't fare well during this turmoil of transporting Tom from the mental hospital every weekend. "She looked young even though she smoked. But from 1975 to her death in 1984, her looks completely changed. She looked like she aged 25 years."

His last memory of his mom is when she showed him the engagement announcement for his cousin Sandy, Jim Miller's daughter. This was January 1975 and Scott says little did he know his mom would soon be gone and he'd be sharing a bedroom at Sandy's house, taken in by her parents.

"Wow," is the reaction of Linda Dooley Johanek, executive director of the Domestic Violence Center in Cleveland, when I call her and tell her about the 1970s allowance of Tom to visit regularly with his children after killing Linda.

"That is just amazing that that happened," says Johanek. "I think I can say fairly confidently that couldn't happen today. If a person is declared insane, it wouldn't be considered safe to let him visit with his children.

"But I'll tell you what, we do have the state's only on-site visitation center where non-resident parents can see their children. These are offenders who have been charged or convicted of domestic violence but they still have rights for visits. The courts and community still see this as vital – to not break parental contact."

Johanek believes society doesn't recognize enough how traumatic domestic violence is for children living in homes where mom and dad are battling it out. "After dad is arrested, it's a tough question for a kid whether to continue the relationship or not. Children do love their parents, no matter what."

Johanek says her center places an emphasis on youth programs and helps children in their shelters deal with the stress in their young lives. "Domestic violence in your home can be life altering for a child. It takes a long time for any kind of healing to happen," she adds.

From the 1970s to 2010, Johanek says it seems crazy that the issue of domestic violence is still strapped by its biggest problem: The public's negative perception of the victim. "Society continues to blame the victim," she says. "I can understand law enforcement getting tired of going to the same houses. But my message for victims is: 'It's not your fault. You deserve better.' We don't need to do anything to increase the shame."

Tom's defense attorney is easily reached in Akron by phone. At age 69, Bradford "Buck" Gearinger offers a crisp, concise account of Tom's case – with a dash of frankness.

"Now that was a tragedy," he begins when I inform him of the reason for the call. "Wow! Almost 35 years ago.

"Tom was truly incompetent to stand trial. It was an insane act with no rhyme or reason. He suffered from mental illness. It's hard to meet someone more off his rocker than Tom."

When he was first hired by Pat and Dominic Sanginiti to talk with Tom in the Summit County jail, he says the defendant "was out of it." Gearinger found it impossible to communicate with Tom about what happened.

Yet the prosecutor wanted a first degree murder charge because the crime was so brutal – all those 13 stab wounds. "But Tom couldn't communicate, appreciate the charge or help me with his defense," recalls Gearinger, who sounds very fired up as he continues to recall the case.

He says his insanity defense was no slam dunk. "Even back then, juries are very reluctant to rule a defendant insane, especially with such a heinous crime like this one."

Gearinger vividly recalls the behind-the-scenes drama of riding over to Lima State Hospital for the Criminally Insane with the assistant prosecutor Gene

King. They wanted to talk with the physician who gave a deposition declaring a "competent and sane" diagnosis of Tom.

"Tom was all but foaming and ranting. I couldn't believe this decision came out of Lima," he says. What he saw shocked the young attorney.

"Lima was like a 19th century dungeon. Thank god, they eventually closed the place," he says. (Lima ran from 1915 to 1982 as a place for the criminally insane; then was turned over to the state for a prison facility).

In his opinion, the physician is not a qualified psychiatrist ("He was a washed-up physician out of Indiana," declares Gearinger, not mincing words). He says that doctor hid from the defense team a report by a trained Cincinnati psychiatrist who found Tom not competent to stand trial.

After reading this in Tom's file, the prosecutor took his view but the charges aren't dismissed.

As an Oct. 17, 1975 *Beacon Journal* article states, Herbert D. McLain pleaded guilty to voluntary manslaughter and was ordered committed to a state mental hospital and then he was to serve seven to 25 years in prison. McLain is sent to Massillon, like Lima also a facility for the criminally insane.

Everything is set legally – all the heartache obviously not close to being healed though. But the prosecutor does recommend the maximum sentence in keeping with the wishes of Linda's grieving family members.

Not so fast. What happened next "shocked" the tough defense attorney.

Chapter Fifteen
Here Comes Tom

Just a couple months after the court showdown, Tom came strolling into his defense attorney's office.

"He was an outpatient!" exclaims Buck Gearinger. "Many visits followed and he was either jazzed up on drugs or so sedate, he could barely walk through the door."

Gearinger says he found it unbelievable that Tom is released from Massillon State Hospital, founded in 1898 and not far from Akron, into the community. This went on for about five years until Tom kills himself.

"He had very little control and no supervision," he says. At the time, Massillon is lauded for its "cottage design" where patients live away from the immense castle-like buildings on the grounds.

Gearinger says Pat Sanginiti, Tom's mom, is very emotionally involved with her son. As the regional director for Fashion 220 cosmetics at the time of her death, she is no push-over. "She wanted this freedom and I guess she got it," he says.

Yet he couldn't keep the gruesomeness of the crime out of his mind. "Only a crazy man would have done this."

He tries to tell Tom this walking about town is a two-edged sword. "Hey, the only defense I had was insanity. I kept it going as long as I could but with him home on weekends, he was going to soon face serious jail time."

Right before Tom was due back in court in the spring of 1980, he ended it all with the pill overdose. "That was the end of my dealings with the family," says Gearinger.

"How do people rise out of those kind of tragedies? Even after all these years, I don't have an answer."

My PGA office buddy Margaret Garforth lives to age 73, dying in 1993 of a myriad of health problems, which began in 1977, two years after the tournament.

I find her daughter, Lee Ann Weisenmiller, mentioned in her father's obituary which details Raymond Garforth's death on Jan. 23, 2008.

A quick online check and I discover Lee Ann is treasurer of the Coventry School system, serving the scenic Portage Lakes area next to Akron.

Lee Ann, as a top administrator, is much too busy to chat during the work week so I call her on a Saturday.

"Linda's death really shook my mom up pretty good," she says, adding that she remembers my connection to her mom.

At the time, Lee Ann is 27, the same age as Linda. And Lee Ann, then a stay-at-home mom, would bring her blonde-haired daughter, Ramona, age 4, into our downtown office on occasion to see Margaret.

Margaret dotes on her family, Lee Ann mentioning her parents met in the ninth grade.

Lee Ann herself starts working in 1977 and after furthering her education, ends up serving 30 years in the

Coventry School system. She retires and then continues to be treasurer because the state of the economy makes it cheaper for the system to retain her than hire an expensive replacement.

"My mom tended to be extra judgmental," she says when we talk about Margaret's distaste for J. Edwin Carter. "She didn't like many of her bosses." But I add that she was also spunky – a word not used much today.

"That she was. I like to think I inherited that trait because if something needs to be done, I roll up my sleeves and tackle the project," she says.

Lee Ann, 62, gives an example that because of budget cuts, she had to let go the woman cleaning her office so it's not unusual for her and her staff to get out a mop and dust rag.

That was so like Margaret, short, blonde and opinionated. When we walked into those PGA offices on Day One, we were greeted with a roomful of boxes and only promised electric typewriters and desks.

Margaret wasn't one to sit around. She whipped the office in shape and as our supplies and furniture arrived, she wouldn't tolerate clutter. Everything was put in its place.

Lee Ann says she recently found the gold PGA name badge we all wore on our Izod dresses. And she remembers coming to the white trailer at the golf course where we worked the last few weeks of our tournament job.

"It's funny Mom never golfed," she says. "It was an odd job for her but she was very good with her office skills."

I remembered that Margaret smoked in the office then as well as M.J. Carter. I smoked but never in the office. For years, I had one or two cigarettes at night after the kids were in bed.

It's strange to picture that PGA office. While downtown Akron might be alien to me now, I would still feel somewhat at home taking a stroll, I think. But back then, I was part of the normality of the place, the rhythm, the people going to and from work. I no longer hold an easy perspective of what life is like. But I am happy to live and celebrate all that I have in family and friends.

I have no plans to go to my 45th high school reunion in October. I had already been back to Ohio twice in 2009 for my mom's graveside service in May and a family reunion in June. I'll keep thinking about going though because I do like fall.

But I do dislike that people in high school know me as "Perv." Our family grew up with the surname of Perv. With today's illicit notations, research is done to try to change the family name.

My cousin, Ron, an artist in Jupiter, Fla., and his son, Dan, a former grade school assistant principal and now a school textbook supplier living in Jacksonville, come up with evidence Perv is not our name. We are the Parvus. They found the name is changed from Parvu at Ellis Island in the early 1900s when my grandfather gets off the boat from Romania, via Italy.

So at my family reunion, we have half Pervs and then those who've changed their name to Parvu. This is frightening to think our whole heritage is wiped away with a government authority's pen. But then our ancestors came from Transylvania – we have resilient Romanian blood cursing through our Parvu bodies.

Whatever my maiden name, Akron has made me what I am and my quest after living there has been to just be who I am. I know this about myself. I'm not a social butterfly by any means.

One thing that's vivid in my mind is Akron's high society side, especially rearing its head during my Betty Jaycox days when this newspaper editor made me help her cover the charity event "Day at the Races." It was a who's who at the horse track, located close to Cleveland, and I dress in a straw wide-brim hat, pink A-line dress, pale hose and a pink coat. I thought I looked very upper crust with all that matching going on.

At the golf tournament, most of the volunteers I ran into had money from husbands with lucrative careers. They went to these kind of charity events such as the "Day at the Races." They played golf, hired child care, attended cocktail parties. I can't say all were high society by Akron's definition but it was definitely the west side crowd. Because everybody knows everybody, sometimes the first question asked is, "Where did you grow up," as a way to separate the wheat from the shaft, I guess. You don't think of the home of manufacturing tires as having a social structure. But the culture was such it made me always stop and take notice when I bumped elbows with Akron society.

My burning tire dump background is not what the Akron trendy set is looking for with that query about pedigree. When I did the Merriman Road story in 1976, a year after the PGA came to Firestone, people were not happy I actually had the nerve to reveal here's where the rich people live – as if we all lived in harmony and equality.

The working class in Akron did have its well-off preachers. The clergy lived rather high on the hog, as if to "share" their wealthy status with worshippers. But that's the closest most factory workers got to big money. When my son took me to Mackinac Island for a 2009 summer vacation, I noticed Akron's TV evangelist Rex Humbard listed on the restaurant Woods' menu as donating the stained glass windows.

I e-mail my former husband Larry; he covered religion in Akron as well as labor and business. "Is there where Rex took those rubber factory dollars and played in somewhat seclusion?" I write.

"Hi. I was thinking about your e-mail and I began to recall that Rex Humbard did have longtime ties with Mackinac Island," answers Larry. "Part of that at everyone else's expense. I fondly remember that wonderful *Beacon Mag* piece you did on who lived on Rex's street. Great, great feature and laid out like a Monopoly board. Boy, did you stir up a hornet's nest with that one. I was proud of you."

I write: "It was Merriman Road. Remember I wore my PGA Izod dress to do interviews because I thought that made me look professional?"

Larry writes, "The pro you were. Going undercover with PGA garb was smart."

Well, I didn't go undercover but I'll grab that praise from Larry, who doesn't hand it out so easily.

In his "My Story," Nicklaus writes about why his marriage to fellow Ohioan Barbara Bash is such a success.

They mark 50 years on July 23, 2010. "Both of us come from uncomplicated, hardworking, down-to-earth, closely bonded Midwestern families."

I know what he's talking about but I doubt the uncomplicated part. Margaret Garforth's daughter tells a very complicated story of her parents' sliding into the abyss of bad health and ensuing loneliness. After her mom died, Lee Ann watched her dad buy a sports car and try to date for the first time in almost 60 years. A native of Britain with a slight accent, he was later the hot commodity at both the assisted living facility and nursing home.

Lee Ann says something a bit weird I can totally identify with. She says her mother had to get out of the way (through death) in order for Lee Ann to get to know her dad. In my family, my dad was the forceful person so my mom's interests always came second. But when my dad died, my mom's mind and body are frail. Still, little fragments of what would be her interests came out. My mom wasn't real talkative in her later years but she took up reading Westerns and watching John Wayne movies with a vengeance. She played a mean set of dominoes and didn't like to lose – a competiveness I didn't know she possessed. She found what she loved to do.

Here's what I wonder about the most. Tom and Linda lack a secure, warm marriage. The fighting took its toll. If Tom and all his problems hadn't been in the picture – if he and Linda had divorced or he just left – what would Linda's life been like? I truly believe, I saw a very rare glimpse of that early on in our PGA job where I witness Linda emerging as a confident young woman. This is one of her first real work experiences with potential because the PGA would have been a great reference. She is struggling to get her bearings but she is honestly trying.

This is real life in all its messy, sometimes confusing state, whether you are Midwestern or not.

Chapter Sixteen
Back to Akron

I call one of my best friends from high school (Kenmore Class of '64) who went to Ohio State and recently retired as a nurse. Merry Dawn Thompson Kostko isn't attending the October high school reunion because she has a wedding to go to. But she tells me class president George Theodore will be there.

Theodore, who I remember for his good-looking Bulgarian heritage appearance and playground marble skills, has been a friend since kindergarten. We kid each other at reunions that he and I are the longest-lasting friends we both have in our lives. I miss him a lot.

So I book a cheap Air Tran airline ticket and plan to go back to Akron. To walk the downtown streets and see what all has changed. To have fun at my reunion, get caught up and spend time with my sister and friends. Why don't I check out Merriman Road?

I call Firestone Country Club on a Saturday morning in September 2009 to see if it's possible to make a lunch reservation. I know it's a private club. But the website says there's a nine-hole public course now.

"Good evening, Firestone Country Club," says the young male receptionist.

"Ah, actually, it's morning," I tell him playfully.

"Oh yeah, I worked last night so I still haven't made the switch."

He's not sure if I can lunch there or not and I'm told to call during the week, not on weekends when there's a skeleton crew. Then before he hangs up, he says, "Have a good evening."

Better make that switch, buddy.

One thing I learned from my newspaper days is always go straight to the top. So after a Tuesday morning phone call where the Firestone receptionist shoots down my having lunch at the club, I send an e-mail to Manager Mark Gore.

I'd just like to stroll down memory lane, I tell him, adding that I worked for the 57th PGA Championship. So having played the "old lady" card, I wait for his response. I did inform him too I was working on a young woman memoir.

"We would love to have you," Gore e-mails me back. "We do not take lunch reservations but you would not have a problem finding a table. I look forward to meeting you."

Back in Florida, my husband, Ray, and I are summer members at Isla Del Sol, a yacht and country club down the street. The seven-month fee is $550 and we join every year because I can golf the back nine and the granddaughters can swim in the enormous pool by Boca Ciega Bay.

I tell the pool bartender John, I'm going to lunch at the mother lode of all country clubs – Firestone. He is impressed. Then I bet him (a drink, maybe) that Firestone won't have any sandwiches over $10 on its lunch menu. "I don't know about that," he says dubious. "But it's Akron!' I counter.

With all this Akron thinking, I wonder if the Massillon State Hospital for the Criminally Insane is still serving lunch. It's not, says a receptionist at the Massillon Chamber of Commerce.

She tells me on the phone the hospital closed about 20 years ago; some of the facility actually burned down. And yes, indeed there was a campus-like atmosphere with cottages and a chapel. This was located about 25 miles south of Akron.

Margy Vogt, Massillon Museum public relations director, says not much of the old buildings still exist on the hospital grounds. In 1989, Heartland Behavioral Healthcare took over and operates about 130 beds with 265 employees in a new building.

When it was the Massillon State Hospital, Vogt says, there was always a lot of back and forth between the city and hospital. Looking at old photographs online, the place looks stunning. There are a number of medieval castles with turrets and arched porches like in a rich landlord's communal. She says town residents in the early 1900s up until the 1950s used the trolley system to go to the hospital grounds for concerts and picnics. "The gardens were beautiful," says Vogt. An old newspaper clipping found online backs this up; it's titled, "A View of the Beautiful Grounds of the Massillon State Hospital for the Insane."

While she says the cottage design always housed patients who could "possibly function," the hospital took even bolder moves in the 1970s when they would release patients on weekend passes and/or to live in group homes. "The philosophy there seemed to be, 'Go live downtown' because we had an awful lot of group homes in Massillon."

Massillon in Stark County, next to Akron's Summit County, isn't widely known for its psychiatric services though. Instead, the town is high school football crazy. The home of actress Lillian Gish and David Canary (the white haired guy on "All My Children"), the place of 30,000 residents today has a stadium that holds almost 20,000. The Massillon team has 22 state football titles and is third in the U.S. in high school victories. A website for the team clicks down to game time: 7 days, 7 hours, 10 minutes, 18 seconds, for example.

No telling if Tom McLain ever took in a high school football game. He more likely high-tailed it to Akron for his many visits whenever he was given leave from Massillon State Hospital.

In the yet another small world category, the Massillon Tigers on Sept. 18, 2009 beat Akron's Firestone High School 42-21.

In preparing for my Akron trip, I look up a *SI Vault* feature online. It's pretty cool to look up the cover of the Aug. 18, 1975 *Sports Illustrated* story about the 57th PGA Championship.

The photo is one of Nicklaus in these god-awful plaid pants bent over his club. The headline: "Aw. Come On Jack. Nicklaus Picks Up Another PGA."

The story "Swinging on a Star" by Dan Jenkins is amusing but it seems so funny that back then media types would file stories for publications that appeared 10 days after an event. This was way before online reporting where articles are written and read by the public before the grass bounces back at a tournament.

Jenkins writes knowingly about the significance of the 16th hole shot. And later in the story, he elaborates in a long sentence, "In winning for the sixth time at Firestone (he has taken the World Series there four times and the American Golf Classic once) and in adding $45,000 to the near $300,000 he won in Akron previously, thus bringing him up to second place behind Raymond Firestone in local earnings, Jack calmly and not so calmly shot rounds of 70,68, 67 and 71 for a total of 276. The most fascinating statistic involved poor Crampton, who finished second in a major championship for the fourth time in his career, and each time Nicklaus was the winner."

The Raymond Firestone moneybags to whom Jenkins refers is the chairman of the tire company at the time plus he is honorary chairman of the 1975 PGA.

His office provides a welcoming letter published in the 1975 PGA book but I never saw Raymond personally. When Linda is murdered, the outreach to our office from any higher ups other than Guster and a few of the Roetzel & Andress lawyers is non-existent. And then for a sports writer of Jenkins' caliber, who looks under every shrub to not mention anything murderously amiss leading up the PGA Championship, probably wouldn't happen today. I wish the cliché, "It was a different time" isn't appropriate here.

Raymond Firestone, who died in 1994 at age 86, left a wonderful legacy to Akron. While his father founded the rubber company and opened Firestone Country Club as a private club, Raymond Firestone's name is attached to a public nine-hole course in the same area. This small course features 3,008 yards of golf and a par of 35. This public facility opened in 1996 and ClubCorp also manages the property.

Firestone family spokesman Troyer says Raymond was the last of the Firestones to live in Akron. "He mostly stayed in Southern Pines, North Carolina later in life," says Troyer. But he was attached to Akron as the last of Harvey Firestone Sr.'s five sons to serve in management of the company.

In 1988, Firestone was bought by Bridgestone Corporation, headquartered in Tokyo as the world's largest tire and rubber company.

So lots of changes to absorb for me who left town when the going got rough.

Chapter Seventeen
Shaping Up the Akron Agenda

To find out more information about Massillon State Hospital for the Insane, I call the local library and am given the number for the hospital's spokesperson Ken Johns.

I'm entertaining the idea of driving to this place that had Tom's care in its hands for five years. But I'm not sure an insane facility would allow me to walk around.

No problem, says Johns, who's very warm and caring on the phone when I fill him in on the particulars but not the specifics of Linda's murder and Tom's case. He uses the phase, "That's a shame" over and over.

Actually, the Heartland name for the institute is just that. The Criminally Insane part of the Massillon Hospital is dropped from the name in 1990. And then the Heartland tag takes over in the late 1990s. "This name more reflected the times," says Johns who's worked there since 1985. So unlike what the Chamber of Commerce told me, it's the same state run place with a different identity and new look but not quite.

Some of the ornate architecture is gone, he says. Still standing are the superintendent's house which resembles a Tudor country house and McKinley Hall with an elaborate theater plus a church-size chapel. Gone is the administration building that looked like a castle and looming brick water tower.

Two of the cottages where Tom spent time still exist but they are under a different state jurisdiction. They house drug and alcohol recovery programs.

In the 1970s, there are weekend passes and lax group homes. There is a Seagull Individual Living Program like Tom is in. And yes, some of the patients probably did go to Massillon football games.

Johns confirms all this, adding it's "a shame in looking back." But today, Tom would not have such freedom to dine with his family and come and go as easy as a breeze to Akron.

"In most cases, there's little visitation with a family until a patient is discharged," Johns says. Then he elaborates, "A different case altogether is someone declared incompetent to stand trial. They are almost always restricted to the facility. If the person's mental capacity can be restored, then it's a goal to work toward that. But if someone is accused of committing a crime, the court would be their next step."

Johns says there are so many layers of restrictions that any increase in privileges has to go through court approval. "The treatment team, the activity therapist – all these people and more have to approve a patient being allowed any outside activity. In a crime situation, even a forensic review team weighs in."

He says at one time patients did have more freedom to come and go. But in listening to a few more details about Tom's case, he expresses shock.

When I mention the Seagull Individual Living Program, he agrees with me that this is a very '70s name as well as concept. "I've heard older employees talk about that. So if he were in that, he would have had more and more privileges.

"It's a shame," he says again. "I can see where his weekend passes would cause a real wedge in the family, not to mention what this did to his children."

Even with all the court cautions, he says, it happens today that families are split down the middle about having a mental patient released. "You have to remember, there's been a lot of heartbreak whether there's been a crime or not."

As for the Massillon football games, Johns says patients don't go now. "It's a matter of finances and staffing. The state has cut back a great deal." But there was a day when such field trips were the norm.

The fall of 2009 marks something new for this city's football powerhouse. The school plays three Akron high schools. Besides Firestone from the fancy suburb, Buchtel and Garfield from inner city neighborhoods are opponents.

"I can't imagine patients going to Massillon's games," I say. "Especially someone involved in an ultra-violent knife attack."

Then I ask if there are guards at Heartland or could I just drive in if I wanted to take a stroll during my upcoming Akron visiting.

"Sure, you can visit the grounds," he says.

And perhaps I shall.

Another place I'd like to go is Ellet High School. Tom is Class of '60 and Linda is '65. I have secured yearbook photos in the past but I would like to eventually talk to some of their classmates to figure out the ill-fated couple's youth potential.

I've already chatted briefly with Florida engineer Philip Souers. I find him, Class of '65, in a jiffy. The city of Akron's website has a link to one of those alumni sites where you sign up to find classmates at various schools. Only this one has a listing I can look through. I can only look for males with unusual names in hopes of reaching someone because women usually change their last names when marrying.

So I spot Souers Ellet 1961-65. I find another listing of him as a donor to the University of Akron's engineering college. And then he is mentioned in a story about Siemens Westinghouse Power in the Orlando area. From these clues, I locate his home phone number.

Souers says I'm lucky to find him at home. He's recovering from a hernia operation. He has never heard of this tragedy of Tom murdering Linda. He knew both, although Tom just as a basketball player at his alma mater.

He says of their 450 students at Ellet, Linda stood out because she was "a popular individual."

"I enjoyed her fellowship," he says quite formally. Poor guy, I didn't mean to break this sad news to him. I thought word of her death would have spread in Linda's class. But Souers says he doesn't go to reunions although there are some Ellet classmates in Florida he's in touch with. "I just don't think news of her death ever circulated," he says.

"Linda was very nice. She was in some of my advanced classes so I viewed her as intelligent," he adds.

He says she was soft spoken and he remembers her singing in the choir.

I mention that the murder happened after Tom is laid off from Firestone. "I think it (the murder) was probably related to that. Too much stress, " he says. Then, he pauses for a moment to think. "Of course, there are other options," he adds.

Souers is familiar with the ups and downs of the tire industry. He worked for two rubber companies, including a summer job like I had delivering mail at Goodyear.

"It's just too bad," he concludes, sounding like he really doesn't want to express his emotions too much to this stranger on the phone. "She was a lovely person."

I came home one night to this e-mail right before my Akron trip. "Temps are chilly here now. I looked on the long term forecast, and temps will be around 60 during the day (65 at most) but 50s and below overnight. So, when packing, plan accordingly. "

It's from my good friend Shirley who's going to Firestone with me for lunch. How did I get so fortunate to have a nurturing friend like her?

My sister rings me shortly after Shirley's e-mail. She tells me their furnace kicked on twice during the night. I guess my Florida thin blood reputation precedes me.

I suggest to my sister we have dinner in downtown Akron after I arrive. "There's nothing there," she replies curtly.

How about Chrissie Hynde's place, I suggest. She nixes that because she's not as intrigued by "VegiTerranean" dining as I would be. I haven't eaten red meat in years, relying on chicken, turkey and seafood and lots of salads and veggie dishes.

Hynde, the hard ass rocker of The Pretenders, wrote "My City Was Gone" in 1982 about Akron. This is right around the time I skedaddled when the factories are closing and jobs are drying up. How can my sister not feel kinship to Chrissie and want to eat at her VegiTerranean restaurant? I tease her.

Akron's Hynde is born Sept. 7, 1951 and my sister shares the same birth date, only one year older. But this still doesn't budge my sis. She's not taking me to VegiTerranean even though I'm thinking to myself, she could order pasta.

I receive a rather interesting call the night before I depart for Akron. It's from Tom Robinson, who graduated from Ellet with Linda. He is given my name and number by Philip Souers whom I reached at home earlier.

Robinson says, "I vaguely remember Linda." He cites a precise number of 432 students in their Ellet class.

He lived right by the high school and was active in marching band and Boy Scouts. He admits he was quiet in high school and passes on more names for me to pursue.

Robinson lives in Palm Harbor, about a half hour from where I live. I don't have to break the news to him about Linda's death because Souers has already done so. He tells me about a terrible tragedy that occurred at Ohio State when he was a student there. A woman set fire to one of the 24-story dormitories, injuring many people. The arsonist never serves any time either, he says, adding that Tom's freedom after killing Linda doesn't surprise him. "That insanity plea gets plenty of people off the hook," he reasons.

Robinson says he's been to every class reunion since the 30th but he can't recall Linda's name being on the roster of the dead. "When they are reading that list, I'm usually frozen with emotions when I hear somebody's name I knew well," he says, adding that a trumpet playing buddy Louis Putt's death came as a big shock to him at the last reunion.

"They never say how a person died," he adds.

He remembers Victor McLain, Tom's brother, who was in his class. Victor McLain came to Robinson's house for Cub Scouts as Robinson's mother was den mother. "He had black hair – of Italian descent," he says of the McLain teen.

Did they all hang out at the Pogo, that drive-in restaurant where Linda eventually meets Tom?

"That's where the wild kids went like Victor but really what's the definition of 'wild' from back then. If a girl smoked in our class, that was supposed to mean she was having sex."

Robinson, who worked for Corning Glass and now is a consultant in the medical industry, has one unsettling memory of Victor McLain. During a class reunion casual get-together at East Gate Bowling Lanes, male and female law enforcement officers show up. They are strippers. This is a gift from Victor McLain, says Robinson. McLain is working in Orlando with a landscape company and can't make the reunion. "Everyone commented about how this was in such poor taste," says Robinson.

Chapter Eighteen
Akron Is Intriguing – Totally

My flight is late arriving in Akron so I watch the colorful crimson tree tops, rolling landscape dotted with water towers and dull gray clouds. I'm excited to see foliage and express this to the retired Akron schoolteacher sitting next to me on the airplane. She retorts, "What's so great about death?" Huh? I mention I keep a tacky vase of fake leaves on my dining table in Florida every autumn to pretend fall is surrounding me. She adds something about cold weather stopping photosynthesis, making the leaves die.

Oh well, I'm thinking other thoughts as I land.

I had hoped to scoot off to Ellet High School on Thursday afternoon, Oct. 1, 2009. But since I am in my sister's car and it is almost 3 p.m., I figure the language arts teacher I had been in touch with would have been already gone. I called Steve Pryseski anyway and leave a message in case he is staying late but he doesn't call me back. So I scrapped going to the school to pick up 1960 and 1965 yearbooks until Friday.

With Linda out of high school for only nine years when she is killed, I figure I might have some luck in finding people who knew her and could fill me in on what she is like. The same for Tom. I hadn't talked to anyone in his class yet.

On my way to my sister's home for a brief stop to drop off my carry-on bag, I see examples of Ohio weird.

Now Ohio weird is different from Florida weird in that in the Sunshine State we don't pay any attention because Florida is wall-to-wall weird – that is unless you are a reporter desperate for a story.

But in Ohio, it sticks out. First, I spot a basement house. Visually, it's difficult to describe this structure except to say it's a basement with a staircase door on top of the flat tar roof. Built after World War II to ease the housing crunch, most basement home dwellers have finished theirs by adding an upstairs "house." Not this one though.

Next sight we see as we cruise along is Officer Dummy, a mannequin law enforcement officer sitting in a cruiser by the side of the road. This fake cop is to deter speeders.

And finally, there is a home with a circular driveway where two huge tractor tires have been cut in half and used as markings on the entrance and exit. The four tire pieces have been painted white and turned upside down so the roundness sticks in the air, offering a reflective guide into or out of the driveway.

My sister thinks I'm being weird myself in pointing out these sights. She's simply used to Ohio – how it smells, how it looks, how it feels. But I drink it all in like for the first time.

Later, my sister provides a driving tour of modern day Akron. No obvious weirdness here. I haven't been downtown since leaving in 1982, no doubt with "My City Was Gone" blaring in my consciousness.

Unlike that Hynde song though ("There was no downtown" wail the lyrics), there is a downtown but it's shabby looking. As we enter the outside rim, I see some former Goodrich red brick smokestacks. These relics from the past are now part of a recycle center that supplies power to downtown.

There's also an impressive Vernon Odom Boulevard wrapping around downtown. Larry and I knew Odom well. Larry was on the board of the Urban League where Odom, the son of a former slave, was executive director.

Downtown is the site of two huge hospitals, Akron General where I and my children were born and Children's where my son at the age of two has eye surgery to correct a "lazy eye" condition.

So there are lots of medical jobs still here. But it doesn't take too long a tour to determine that the two driving forces behind downtown are the University of Akron where I taught feature writing briefly in 1982 and The Chapel church where I freelanced during the 1970s.

This school and church take up a lot of land, including the former Polsky's department store on Main Street, now devoted to UA classroom space. When I used to work at Polsky's during college, I had great difficulty in tying big cardboard boxes full of clothes with string. But I loved buying "mod" clothes at discount.

The Chapel, 135 Fir Hill St., has grown to nine acres in this area, including a gymnasium and urban outreach program.

I think the expansion of the hospitals, UA and The Chapel make Akron unique. Most downtowns would love to have such viable institutions.

Downtown has Canal Park, where a minor league baseball team plays, and a park – not there when I worked downtown. Akron Aeros, the minor league team of the Cleveland Indians, play in a faux historic brick stadium next to the former O'Neil's department store. My sister says it's cool to go to a game there when they play the bouncy tune "YMCA" because you can look out at the truly historic YMCA building still downtown.

The former Portage Hotel is now occupied by SummaCare, an insurance and health care company. In 2003, SummaCare decided to honor the history of the United Rubber Workers founded in 1935 at the Portage Hotel, on the corner of Main and Market streets. (History footnote: The URW merged with the United Steelworkers of America in 1995).

There's a URW commemorative garden plus an Ohio historical marker. There are also engraved bricks which can be purchased to honor past URW members who once formed a mighty union that represented all the tire factory workers.

Alcoholics Anonymous was founded up the street in the lobby of the former Mayflower Hotel where Bill W. made that first call for help to quit drinking. It's now Mayflower Manor where seniors and those with disabilities can rent inexpensive apartments.

So with all this going on why does Akron look so disconnected? I told my sister Akron needs a make-over. Call in a HGTV-like designer to pull a style together, I announce. She says that will not happen with police and firefighters recently being laid off.

Before more downtown touring, we swing down Merriman Road, a few miles from downtown.

The reason I have an interest in this area is because my 1976 story when I wore my PGA dress neatly summarizes a different class in Akron at the time. I know blue collar having grown up where dinner is carried to the table at 5:30 sharp and my dad then leaves to put up TV antennas to supplement his Goodrich factory job.

But Linda's children in 1975, as Scott McLain explains, went abruptly from a working class home next to a belching tire factory to ritzy Fairlawn, where upper middle class and just plain rich people lifestyles are the norm. The Millers also belong to Portage Country Club, a quick trip from Merriman Road., like Scott said.

So before I left for Akron, I asked the *Akron Beacon Journal* to hunt down the Merriman Road article. It is mailed to me a few days before my departure. I want to review what I wrote to better understand the changes in the McLain children's lives.

I admit I was fascinated by this big Tudor thing (okay, mansions) of Akron when I wrote the story. I have since seen a lot of gigantic residential spreads, including the leafy estates in the Grosse Pointes where the auto industry giants grew wealthy.

But back then I was a sponge taking it all in as I walked Akron's version of an Avenue of Conspicuous Consumption. The thing about Merriman Road is it is so visible – not a gated community – but on a very well-traveled road.

Well-manicured lawns run two to three acres from Sunnyside to Monmouth drives where I profiled 36 families.

"If you'd guess them (the residents) to be an idle nobility, sitting on fat fortunes accumulated by rubber-baron fore bearers, you'd be mostly wrong," I observed.

No, instead I found a variation of the working class just like the Millers. The Merriman people depended on income to pay the enormous heating bills, yard work costs and country club tabs.

The difference from my growing up days is these breadwinners are top management, arriving home at 7 or 8 at night for dinner (we ate "supper"). Then there is a host of business trips, keeping daddies away even more.

Homes in 1975 started at $100,000. At the time Rex Humbard Jr. had three children and lived in a pseudo-Tudor built in 1974 for $134,000. (His TV pastor dad lived nearby on Portage Path).

Always one who loves local history, I noted that in 1837, Charles Merriman purchased the 263 acres which now make up Akron's entire west side for $1,200.

But in 1975, the yards are no longer true showcases full of pachysandras and flowering shrubs, residents lamented to me.

Residents complained yard care could be as high as $363 a month. To clean a house on Merriman cost $20 to $23 a day and yes, I heard that "good help is hard to find" comment more than once.

Cleaning algae from the pool, polishing ornate cherry woodwork, replacing a pane of leaded glass, spiffing up marble on the fireplace hearth – these were chores foreign to our family. My mom scrubbed our linoleum floors on her hands and knees with Fels-Naptha soap. With all this work, why did people stay in these old homes? Suburbs such as Fairlawn, Bath and Silver Lake with newer homes were growing increasingly popular.

But people told me they liked the public school, King School, which incidentally is where the first Alcoholic Anonymous meeting is held outside the Mayflower Hotel.

A banker says, "You get a lot of bang for your buck here." He meant a nice neighborhood plus a monster house.

The ride from Merriman Road is seven minutes (about three and one-half miles) to downtown. And finally, people like the "Lebensraum" or living space aplenty in an old house. You get at least four bedrooms, formal dining room, breakfast area, kitchen, living room, study, multi-baths, library, two car garage, swimming pool and bathhouse.

Social life consists of cocktail parties and formal dinners. But the neighbors say they don't run back and forth for coffee like we did (or rather, the women in my family took Pepsi breaks).

I guess the funniest statement I reported is from a woman who told me that neighbors aren't that keen on mixing because the time a couple has for socializing is reserved for people who'll do their business some good.

Merriman Road still looks good today. Online I found a house for sale at 841 Merriman Rd. for $1.35 million. That money buys six bedrooms, three full bathrooms plus two half baths and 5.18 acres.

Who wouldn't want to live on this treed street? I'm sure houses on this leafy stretch are at prices these Merriman Road residents haven't seen in years.

The street is awfully busy with traffic. My sister has to turn the car around at nearby Sand Run Metro Park because vehicles are zooming by. No imposing gates here on houses. Even the grandest house is easily gawk-able – 1010 Merriman Road called The Anchorage. I wrote a larger profile on this nine-bedroom house because it was the second largest in Akron next to nearby Stan Hywet, now a tourists' showcase in Akron.

In 1975, The Anchorage and its three acres has just been bought by an Akron real estate executive for $70,000 but the former P.W. Litchfield home, the late Goodyear board chairman, needed a lot of work.

I saw the property listed online for sale without a price. So I called a listing agent Joanne Owen when I returned home.

She says the owner Jack Jeter, who recently sold his Jeter Systems Corp., an office organizing business, keeps listing and un-listing The Anchorage. But there aren't too many takers in the 9,643 square feet range for the Merriman Road area.

She's having a tough time selling the $1.35 million home at 841 Merriman Road. "Find me a buyer," she teases, adding it's been on the market for one year.

She says the home is designed by architect Roy Firestone, lesser known of the Firestones. But his life did come to light when the late architectural historian James Pahlau lectured on Firestone's "houses of the 1920s" in recent years.

"There's a view of the Cuyahoga Valley in the back that's breath-taking," says Owen.

"Merriman Road remains the most prestigious street in Akron," she adds proudly.

Chapter Nineteen
Blimp Keeps Following Me

The Merriman Road houses look more casual to me from my 1976 experience – one has both Michigan and Ohio State flags in front. But then again I've seen Beverly Hills mansions from my 10 years as a TV critic and the island where I live has some super duper waterfront homes. I'm not jaded, just more familiar with other people's grand lifestyles.

Back in downtown, my sister and I briefly visit my niece who volunteers at the Akron Democratic headquarters. As we exit the car, the blimp "Spirit of Goodyear" floats overhead. I can hear the whirling in the sky.

"Now that's an Akron moment," my sister says.

Back on our tour, we pass the City-County safety building where Larry and I met in the spring of 1967 and we married not so long afterwards.

I am a student at Kent State, taking a reporting public affairs class and we take a field trip to Larry's *Beacon Journal* office at the jail/court complex. I arrive early and Larry has the nerve to ask me to go do some reporting for him. He is busy and he wants me to duck into a courtroom and write down what is about to happen to a murder defendant. The case is continued, I report back to him. "Aahhh, I thought so," he says. Mr. Big Shot, I'm thinking.

That summer, I work at the *Kent Record-Courier* and I'm sitting there drinking a Nehi orange pop when I spy Larry coming in the front door. What the heck is that guy doing here? I'm thinking.

He wants to ask me out, based on my fine reporting, no doubt. It seems only fitting months later to tie the knot in front of a local judge in that jail complex.

My sister and I drive slowly by Cascade Plaza opened in 1961 where the PGA office was housed. It looks tired and dirty, like a once modern complex that hasn't aged well, but there are some newer looking brick sidewalk designs in front.

The Civic Theater, a 1920s palace of a movie house, is still kicking. But the valley-situated park next door with a skating rink, part of the Cascade Locks Park system, probably won't have a display of Christmas trees and holiday vendors because the city is too broke, my sister says with worry in her voice.

We're actually going to dinner at the site of the former O'Neil's where my family shopped. I was allowed to grab a bus from my Kenmore home when I was in seventh grade or so and come downtown to O'Neil's. At the lunch counter, I'd split with a friend a shrimp cocktail, grilled cheese sandwich and Coke. Our tab with tip was $5. We were living large.

Housed in the renovated O'Neil's is the large Roetzel & Andress law firm – the same lawyers who were over in Cascade and gave us the PGA space. There are two restaurants on the ground floor but one, Ohio Brewing, closed the week previous to my visit.

My sister is palpably bitter there is no longer retail in downtown. We both have wonderful memories of shopping at O'Neil's and Polsky's. My factory worker dad spared no expense in always providing the best for us. My mom was a certified shoe-a-holic. Even in her declining years, Peg had boxes and boxes of arch-support footwear.

My sister worked at O'Neil's in the office in the 1970s along with my cousin Ron, who was in the art department. So there is heaps of nostalgia here. When working across the street for Polsky's as a sales clerk, I wore a "Miss J. Perv" nametag.

Downtown, the dingy storefronts and bricked over windows are common. But Akron owes the lack of its total demise to UA as students spill into downtown for its bars and restaurants.

We dine at the Barley House in O'Neil's Main Street space where drinks are half price. I order a Sam Adams Oktoberfest beer but my sister instinctively says she'll pass because she's driving. My cousin's 1963 DUI-inflicted death is still with her too.

My sister recalls that we are now sitting in the fine jewelry department of O'Neil's. We did know these stores like the back of our hand.

Afterwards, I wander out into the lobby of the building where there are old photos of the glory days of O'Neil's. Before reaching the elevators in the back there are glass-like barriers around where the escalators used to be. But you can look down and see in the basement where once many a bargain could be had. The security guard comes by and says the city owns this storage space and then she adds, "This is where LeBron keeps his bikes."

My sister translates for me. Of course, I know of the Akron native basketball super star LeBron James. He has a bicycle give-away program each year where underprivileged children get new wheels. So as the contributions pour in or roll in, the city gives him space for storage.

The Akron Downtown Partnership has a pamphlet at Barley House where it states there are 43 restaurants, 25 bars and clubs, free parking and trolleys running to the new UA stadium on campus. But down on Main Street, it looks less than lively. My sister quips when I read her those stats, "They must be counting the Subways on campus."

On the way home we visit my parents' grave at Greenlawn, in a true gritty working class neighborhood called Barberton known once for Diamond Match, Sun Rubber and Seiberling Rubber, all gone. This is smack dab next to Kenmore where we grew up.

I'm in a relaxed mood so I don't choke up like I thought I would seeing Peg and Pete together in eternity. I also smile because my sister had the cemetery change the engraved roses on their plaque to dogwood like she originally ordered. My parents liked dogwood and it just goes to show you, you have to be tenacious even in matters of death.

I can't help but think how shiny their grave is. It's also close to where my cousin, John Jeffrey Fulea, is buried. My sister and have a ghoulish conversation about how we wish we could talk with him today and fill him in. He was killed days after he turned 21 by a drunk driver and missed his whole adult life.

This reflection in a cemetery requires a follow-up of Big Comfort Right Now (BCRN). This is a phrase my sister and I use to get through life and death. We usually want to go some place familiar and eat something soothing.

I'm in the mood for a Strickland's cone, bought at the 1936 original location, 1899 Triplett Blvd. This is frozen custard supreme, made of cream, eggs and sugar with as little air as possible. For our cones we travel out to the Rubber Bowl area where the Soap Box Derby compound is also housed.

This region is dominated by the suddenly still 30,000 seat Rubber Bowl, a massive stadium. This is where UA played football until fall 2009 when the new facility named InfoCision Stadium opened on its downtown campus.

I tell my sister my memory of the Rubber Bowl is the city series football game played every Thanksgiving morning when I was growing up. We went as a family – although most of the women stayed home to cook.

"All I could think about during the game was how starved I was," I say.

"But a big dinner was being readied at home. You just had to be patient," my sister scolds.

"Noooo," I respond in mock horror.

This area is also where Goodyear blimps used to be housed in an immensely large covered garage complex.

This area explodes with my family history. I can feel the past pushing on my chest practically. Or maybe that's just brain-like pain from eating my frozen custard.

Across from Strickland's is the Akron Fulton Airport Building, an art deco masterpiece, built in 1931. My sister has some young and in-love photographs of my parents, Peg and Pete, taken in the early 1940s in front of this building. Peg has on saddle shoes and looks trim and sharp. Pete is handsome and all over Peg.

Then when I met my husband, Larry, and he asks me out eventually, he wants to hook up after his covering the Soap Box Derby, a mainstay in Akron since 1935. I explain that July 29, 1967 on Saturday is my 21st birthday and I'll be in a Kent bar with Shirley celebrating. So he drives his red Triumph convertible sports car to Kent.

When he arrives at the bar, I ask Larry how his Soap Box Derby story goes – Derby Downs in all its glory with hundreds of kids in homemade racing cars. He teases, "My lead is 'Little Tommy Snot Nose zooms to the finish line.'"

This corny joke still makes me laugh because reporters always have to cover these kind of community perennial events (in Tampa, it's Gasparilla, a drunken parade) and you do get cynical. But perhaps back then, I already drank too many Vodka Collins. Anyway, that is the night of our first kiss.

At Strickland's, the blimp pursues us, putt-putt overhead. The blimp is returning to its new quarters at Wingfoot Lake Airship facility in Springfield. But as I lick my homemade banana frozen custard cone, I'm thinking these Akron moments just keep coming.

Chapter Twenty
Honored to Be at Firestone, Really

Firestone Country Club is decorated just like I remember. Leather furniture and plaid and rusty colors. Jane O'Crowley, member relations director, who gives us a tour before lunch, reassures Shirley and me that the place has indeed been redecorated many times since 1975.

The interior layout of Firestone C.C. is broken up by narrow hallways and small rooms. There is a wonderful dining area called The Terrace where floor-to-ceiling windows lend a panoramic view of the famed South Course. But since it's pouring rain during our visit, our visibility isn't so great.

I wear black Capri pants and a bright green sweater. I want to wear jean capri pants but I know most country clubs banish jeans.

But Firestone doesn't present a formal handshake when entering. It's actually rec room cozy. There are collage portraits in the foyer. O'Crowley says these represent different ambassadors through the years – golfers and others who have acted as hosts for various tournaments. I ask to see Jack Nicklaus and instead much to my surprise and delight, it's a large drawing of his wife, Barbara, with Jack and their sons in smaller size at her side.

O'Crowley tells me immediately of a big change at Firestone. In 1981, ClubCorp bought the 596-acre club and last year, this complex was purchased by KSL Capital Partners of Denver. ClubCorp still has its name on the 170 golf courses it once owned and operated but the investment firm KSL calls the shots.

But she reassures me that it's business as usual. "Our staff stay for many years here," she says, adding Mark Gore, general manager since 2005, began as a bag boy.

Firestone C.C., 452 E. Warner Rd., has three private courses: the 18-hole South Course, the one where Jack Nicklaus lofted over the tree; the North Course which is known for its lakes and streams, and the West Course opened in June 2002. This gives the club 54 holes. The public Raymond C. Firestone, 600 Swartz Rd. on the next street, has a driving range as well as its nine holes. Cost for this course is $20 to $22 in green fees.

O'Crowley says there isn't a swimming pool, tennis courts or workout room. In other words, families wouldn't come on weekends to Firestone C.C. This is strictly golf and more golf and memberships go to individuals with as high as a $12,000 initiation fee.

"People have their golf club and then usually their country club membership," she says casually of a very stratified world.

The rain is really coming down. Shirley and I have to run with umbrellas to get to the front door. But O'Crowley says not to worry, the courses have excellent drainage systems on the big greens. No shifting, washaway sand either. The dense sand used at Firestone stores heat so well you can see steam rising from the bunkers in the morning.

She brings me to an awesome souvenir of the 57th PGA Championship, the last one held at Firestone. It's a wall hanging drawing of the looming water tower out front which looks exactly like a red tee holding a white golf ball. All the players from that 1975 tournament had signed the golf ball for this framed memento.

During a tournament, O'Crowley says tents are easily set up and taken down and there are now permanent buildings housing the Bridgestone staff and media.

I ask O'Crowley about the architecture of the clubhouse and she says 1970s modern. She sticks her head in the office of another staffer and he says ""Falling Waters," referring to the famous Frank Lloyd Wright house. But at 596 acres, it's truly the country club's serene terrain that is the stand out.

I tell her that when I drove around the yellow brick Firestone factory complex near where I used to live, I noticed the Bridgestone name is downplayed. "That's because the Firestone brand is so strong," she says and we both agree that it would be a black day in Akron history if Firestone Country Club ever has a name change.

In a small meeting room dominated by a conference table, there's a photograph of a beaming Jack Nicklaus clutching his 57th PGA trophy. He's wearing a gold Rolex watch and those plaid pants.

Time for lunch in the Grille Room. Before leaving, somehow the subject of the Goodyear blimp comes up with O'Crowley.

O'Crowley, a pretty young brunette, Shirley and I talk about seeing the airship buzzing around Akron. Shirley informs O'Crowley that her former husband, Mickey Wittman, was the public relations man for the Goodyear blimp for years. This refreshes my memory about why she isn't in Akron in the 1970s to help me cope with all the turmoil, including Linda's death, in my life. Shirley is on the road with the blimp, based in Houston.

At lunch, I'd love to have a glass of Firestone brand California chardonnay at $8.75 a glass. But I do want to go to Ellet High School afterwards so I better not smell of wine. (By the way, the Firestone vineyard is sold by the family in California in 2007. But again, that powerful Firestone name lingers on the labels.)

The Firestone salad, a grilled chicken concoction, is $9.75. Salads and sandwiches are almost all under $10. The salad's tomatoes are pale and mealy. Shirley says, "This shouldn't be happening at this time of year." But I like how the chicken is prepared (with grill marks) and then chopped into small pieces for the salad. And I love that my blue cheese dressing comes in a silver gravy boat.

Paul Lazoran, who was manning the Firestone locker room during the 1975 tournament and continues today, stops by our table right when my Chef Mike's special cream of tomato soup arrives.

Lazoran seems awkward about talking with me. I guess O'Crowley pushed him our way and he's reluctant. When I ask him if he knew tournament director J. Edwin Carter, he merely shakes his head "yes." He says the biggest difference besides the winning money going skyward from 1975 to today is that there is mostly a field of 150 players. Back then it was 75 to 85.

Does he get to know the players. "Nah," he says, "they take their money and get out of town." With that, he excuses himself.

(I find out later, I am wrong about Lazoran, whom I'm told by O'Crowley has worked at Firestone in various capacities since he was nine years old. He is actually the assistant pro during the 57th PGA Championship. I thought his name sounded familiar. So when I skim through the program book again, I see him standing by club pro Bobby Nichols. Lazoran looks like a 1970s poster boy – huge, fluffy hair and tight polyester trousers.)

The 1975 locker room as described by then-Manager Ken Beverly in the 57th PGA program has a staff of eight, expanded by the four-man crew usually in place. Beverly says he arranges for one-hour dry cleaning and shoe repair for the golfers. "In a pinch, we can handle alterations on clothing, too."

Beverly uses a blackboard to keep players up-to-date on weather conditions, courtesy of a weatherband radio (this is before the Weather Channel blared on Firestone's present bank of flat screen plasma TVs). Wind, temperature and humidity figures are posted along with forecast notes. It made for a caring atmosphere, showing how Firestone offers some homey touches.

This is true today when you can see your food being prepared like in mom's kitchen. The Grille Room is small and narrow with a glass window with Firestone Country Club written in gold letters across the top. Behind the window, the cooks are slaving away in the heat of the grill. There are green walls, mahogany brown leather chairs, a flat screen TV and a dark brown scroll-design carpet. Diners are given a paper placemat that shows the layout of the three private courses. The South Course, the largest, has 3,698 yards.

All the diners, all male except one woman and Shirley and me, look damp and indeed when we stop at the pro shop on our way out, the salesman says some crazy people will go out in any weather although the courses do close about Oct. 31 for the season.

The lunch bill is $31.63 and includes a 20 percent tip for our efficient waitress.

I remark to Shirley you'd have to be snappy to work here. I say this because Firestone C.C. has some strange rules in my mind. Shirts must be tucked in when playing golf. I'm sorry but golf clubs are usually Beer Gut City. But then the Grille Room at Firestone lets you un-tuck that shirt – I guess so you can order the blue cheese dressing and relax. No cargo shorts or pants. No hats worn backwards. No jeans.

I just adore O'Crowley because she seems genuinely interested in the preserving of the history of the club. She had shown us a glass case where memorabilia from past tournaments is housed across from the pro shop. The 57th PGA book is there but not in nice of condition like the one I have.

I bop into the pro shop. For my son and son-in-law, I buy red Firestone visors at $19 and then save 40 percent off golf shirts, originally $60.

Not that Firestone needs my financial help to keep going but like I tell a newspaper friend when I get back home, it's an honor to be there. She laughs loud and long because newspaper people never talk like this.

I don't tell her for now that I didn't feel that way in 1975. But she's probably already guessing there's a dark side lurking somewhere here.

In Akron, Shirley drives me to Ellet where she waits in the car and I run in to skim through yearbooks from Linda and Tom's senior years. The 1950-built high school is surrounded by two-story nicer homes but the school is terribly plain. I walk right in and stroll among the diverse group of students who all look swell in today's funky fashions.

I finally encounter a teacher hall monitor who asks where I'm going. I say the office and she directs me. In the office, I'm told to go upstairs to Steve Pryseski's class but I'm not given any kind of security pass (in Florida, for my granddaughters, to enter the school the office staff needs to make a copy of your driver's license).

The kids in Pryseski's class are watching a movie. He's a good looking, middle age man with a graying flat top. I'm assuming he'll want me to sit at a desk and look through the 1960 and 1965 yearbooks. But he says take them, return whenever.

On my way out of the school, I find on the hallway floor, an orange ribbon with gold sticker football at the top. It reads: "Orangemen (Ellet) Fry the Falcons (Firestone H.S.). " Cute, pin-on ribbons just like we wore in high school before big games. (Ellet would lose to Firestone 34 to 7.)

Ellet, a small community south of Goodyear Heights right off Interstate 76, has an interesting history. Mary Jane (Minnie) Ellet (1861-1945) grew up on her family farm just outside Akron. They were among the first settlers in this region and so the town of Ellet was named after the family in 1918. Minnie Ellet was a prohibitionist and defender of women's rights. She worked as a writer for the *Beacon Journal* and never let up on her favorite subject – giving women freedom. So she was a farm girl who accomplished a lot – despite the prohibition wash-out.

Speaking of food and wine, I swear my trips to Akron now consist of eating. For dinner, my sister takes me to Belgrade Gardens, 3476 Massillon Road, a place for chicken dinners. Akron and Barberton people have this fixation on these chicken houses where they serve chicken coated in thick, crunchy breading, hot sauce (rice and spicy tomatoes) and thin, greasy fries. The juice oozes from this freshly fried chicken at the first bite. The cost for my regular size dark meat dinner is $10.79. My sister remembers the price for chicken dinners was between $1 and $2 when we were kids. Normally, I'd have a beer to wash this decadent indulgence down but my class reunion is Saturday and I don't want to look puffy-eyed.

Chapter Twenty-One
Criminally Insane Have It Nice

I pick up a rental car because I want my own wheels for Saturday and Sunday. My sister surprises me by saying she'll drive me to the former Massillon State Hospital for the Criminally Insane.

She knows I'm not wild about driving. I didn't get my driver's license until I was 23 when the *Akron Beacon Journal* hired me and told me, learn to drive or lose your job. So I had to take AAA lessons on my lunch hour. Very embarrassing but then Larry bought me a brand new green Volkswagen bug with an automatic stick shift to nudge me along.

The route to Massillon is simple enough from Akron as we head south, passing the Pro Football Hall of Fame, which has been in Canton since 1963. Continuing on the I-77 interstate, we then take the Massillon exit.

After about a 30-minute ride total, we reach the dirt trail leading back to Heartland Behavioral Health Center. There is a roadside dumpy-looking bar called Elbow Room, 1318 Erie St. S. And the health facility after passing some light industry buildings on the same road is at 3000 Erie St. S.

Heartland is a beautiful, modern complex that fits smoothly into a small valley. The facility is a light brick with green trim complex. We see no security. We just drive in and I keep getting out of the car to look at things.

This lack of anyone riding around on a golf cart or walking the beat may explain why in the summer of 2008, three teens are taken into custody for setting fire to a 110-year-old chapel on Massillon's grounds. The demolished chapel, valued at $225,000 according to the *Massillon Independent,* didn't have utilities when the blaze broke out. So it was empty and unused. This was originally a dining hall but was converted to a Protestant and Eastern Orthodox chapel in the 1950s. A gymnasium was later added.

This might have been where Tom, who had a Baptist burial, came to chill.

At the present day site, the older buildings are in the back of the property on a slight hill. No lavish landscaping or ponds of yesterday but the grass is kept trimmed.

We stopped at McKinley Hall and I feel disappointed the building is being left to deteriorate. There are boarded up and broken windows. The place is a gem historically with scrolls on the banister and columns decorated with blocks holding flower carvings. I peep through the glass front door and spot what looks like a light blue ballroom (probably the theater) with a detailed etched white ceiling. Nothing dark and gloomy inside. But how the state of Ohio permits this facility to slide into ruin baffles me.

The superintendent's former house is orange and red brick. It looks like a large gingerbread cottage right out of Hansel and Gretel. I, of course, am bellyaching to my sister and she retorts, "What is Ohio going to do? Rent this out for weddings on the grounds of an insane asylum?"

The house, which looks unoccupied, is full of antique furniture and has incredible stained glass windows. I walk around the back and say to my sister when I return to the car, "The back where I think the gardens must have been is even more enchanting." In the back, the house's whimsical slanted roof is more prominent.

Across the way, we see two cottages where Tom resided after killing his wife. I don't know why they are called cottages because they are large three-story buildings with brick porches. Typical of alcohol and drug rehab patients, people are milling outside these cottages smoking cigarettes.

But no one else is around. The mental health facility is located next to a golf course where we see about a six-foot wire fence separating the two properties. Men are chipping shots right and left.

We stop at the old brick chapel on the grounds. The sign informs it's the National Shrine of St. Dymphna with Fr. Ed Gretcko as the spiritual leader.

Dymphna? I'm stumped. Then my sister's eagle eye sports a small explanation that this is the saint for peace of mind. In back there's a very small glass A-frame structure for private prayer and worship.

"Pretty nice for a someone who murders his wife," I muse outloud as we exit and head to downtown Massillon not even five miles away.

We drive through the downtown residential area off of Lillian Gish Boulevard and I spot something I totally forgot about not living in the Midwest for so long. Almost every block has these taverns. They are dark, dingy hideouts that reek of beer and cigarettes where people go to drown their troubles. These are independent neighborhood businesses where food is usually lacking and I'm surprised there are so many in Massillon. Let's just say I was double surprised there is one so close to Heartland's complex.

"Go Tigers Go" is the downtown's theme with a huge football scene painted on the side of a downtown building. The downtown is in a valley and my sister observes that it looks like there's a lot more to do than in Akron. There's even a shop devoted to high school football gear called "Howard's Tiger Rags."

We lunch at a place called Menches Brothers claiming to have invented both the hamburger and ice cream cone. I am extremely dubious of this but my sister says it's true (with a wink) because the menu says so. The vegetable soup I order is okay but the salad bar is pretty blah. I guess Menches didn't invent the salad bar.

Back home at my sister's, I leaf through 532 pages of Edward Kennedy's "True Compass: A Memoir." Being a good Democratic household, my sister would have this memoir. But then, she always buys the best books. We both read our heads off. It's definitely our shared BCRN.

Being a rabid Cleveland Indians baseball fan, she would also have the latest tome about the Tribe. It's by Phil Trexler and is called, "Cleveland Indians: Yesterday & Today."

I immediately check put pages 82 and 84 where there is information on Tony Horton "who succumbed to mental pressures and quit baseball in the middle of a doubleheader on Aug. 28, 1970."

He was a power-hitting first baseman and poor Tony, I was dispatched by the *Akron Beacon Journal* on Opening Day 1970 to interview him.

The headline of my April 1970 story read: "Hey Girls: Your Dreamboat's Waiting!"

The story began: "Tony Horton has the kind of clear, sky blue eyes that a girl can get lost in. Yet the tall, blond, and disarmingly handsome first baseman says he has trouble finding a date." In the story, Horton, then 25, talked about his idea of a good date: "A movie, dinner, quiet conversation."

Now with *The Plain Dealer* but formerly a *Beacon Journal* sports writer Terry Pluto in his book, "The Curse of Rocky Colavito" about those miserable Indians, wrote of my story, which he dug up from the *Beacon Journal's* archives:

"Obviously they don't write stories like these anymore – and for good reason." But he says I did remind fans that Horton was supposed to be the next heartthrob, yes, another Rocky Colavito.

Whatever "mental pressures" Tony Horton suffered, I'm sure he wasn't helped any by my awful writing as a novice reporter.

What must be the mental pressures at Heartland? When I research Saint Dymphna, it's not a pretty story. This is whom the shrine is named after on the Heartland grounds. Her father was an Irish king who, when his wife died, driven mad by grief and mental illness, made sexual advances toward his daughter. Dymphna ran away to Belgium but was found there by her father. When she refused to come back to Ireland with him, he decapitated her.

Dymphna is the patron saint of those who suffer from mental illnesses, nervous system disorders, epileptics, mental health professionals, incest victims and runaways.

Her burial place in Gheel hosts a world-class sanatorium, according to Wikipedia, the online info guide founded in St. Petersburg, Fla.

The Rev. Gretchko, who's the administrator of the St. Dymphna church at Heartland as well as head of the gothic-looking St. Mary's Catholic Church in Massillon, tells the *Massillon Independent* newspaper in July 2009 that the reason for the record high 11 homicides in Stark County so far this year (there were only nine last year) is, "These events occur without discipline." He says the rejection of God's laws and decline of family are the reasons for a moral lapse. He adds that it's up to mothers and fathers to instill values in their children.

Linda's children are minus one mother because of one father who's also gone forever from their lives.

I try reaching the Rev. Gretchko to talk with him about his ministry at Heartland but his secretary is a Nosey Parker. And I can tell by her dubious tone and questions, she's deciding he probably won't bother to call me back.

Chapter Twenty-Two
In High School, Give Me a Break

As I get ready for my high school reunion, I think about how self-confident I feel as opposed to my younger days. I have worked for five newspapers, *Kent Record-Courier, Akron Beacon Journal, St. Petersburg Times, Des Moines Register* and *Tampa Tribune,* over a 40-year span.

Yet if two people hadn't cared about my future in high school, none of this may have happened. I had no plans and no money to go to college. There is the Romanian background holding me back. In the Old Country, there's an age-old respect for men; Romanian women come second. I see this daily in my extended family where men call all the shots. It's not like we go around speaking our native tongue or wearing Old World duds, although my grandfather dresses in the black garb of foreigners all his life. The problem for me is the women in my family are all so darn domestic. I can't sew a men's sports jacket; my sister can and does.

Fortunately, a career for me shapes up. As editor of my high school newspaper, *The Kenmore Cardinal,* I become a *Beacon Journal* teen reporter, filing tidbits to *Beacon* staffer Nancy Yockey Bonar. I end up even cleaning her apartment for loose change. She calls my high school journalism teacher, Tony Marano, and together they come up with a Northeastern Ohio Scholastic Press Association scholarship for me that pays for my freshman year at Kent State.

I am so nervous in asking my dad if I could go to college. It's springtime 1964 and the clock is ticking on my readying myself for such a huge life change. Finally, I tell my dad all about it. He says breezily, "Why not? It's free." Big relief and my mom later drives me to the campus for student orientation.

If Linda had just gotten such a similar lucky break, she could have landed a good job as a secretary or who knows what else.

But she meets Tom too soon before she can make that leap. After graduation and then marriage a few months later, she quickly has Scott the next year, one year after school, and then Jody a year later. She is busy on the home front, and even busier when Kara comes along eight years after her graduation.

My high school reunion is low-key with about 60 classmates out of 300-plus in attendance. The Saturday event is at the Polish American Citizens Club, and Sunday's lunch is at Allenside Athletic Club, well-worn places where a beer is $1.50 and mixed drinks are $1.75.

The menu Saturday is sliced beef, Polish sausage, chicken cordon bleu, green beans, au gratin potatoes, salad and rolls. Sunday's is broasted chicken, Jo-Jos (fried potatoes) and cole slaw.

I pick the bacon out of the cordon bleu dish and eat a few beans and some salad. On Sunday, I peel the skin off my chicken and eat one Jo-Jo.

At the reunion, many of us share health stories, talking about Social Security benefits and retirement activities. Thirty-one classmates out of the 300-plus have died and that certainly sets a pall over the festivities.

There is no band and classmate Peter Carpenter, a urbane Clevelander, promises he will personally hire a band for our 50th.

But then who wants to dance? I hug George Theodore.

Theodore, who's naturally gregarious, works the room like it's an insurance convention. He talks freely and I marvel at his full head of curly hair, tinged with gray but still black.

I am a little self-conscious about wearing a name tag "Janis Perv" to go with my V-neck orange sweater and black fall leaf patterned skirt.

I tell Theodore my maiden name is now Parvu and he says his Bulgarian family name was changed also at Ellis Island. But he'll keep the Theodore because he stumbles pronouncing the Bulgarian version. He graduated from Ohio University and owns Yellow Jacket T-shirt company in North Akron. Five years earlier he gave all of us Kenmore High Class of '64 T-shirts at the reunion. But like I said to my sister, "Who would go around wearing a shirt announcing you are that old?" He has an attractive wife, two pre-teen daughters and a seven-year-old son. "A lot to live for," he says, smiling, his ever-present white teeth showing.

Karl Auker, a football playing hottie in high school, lives near Napa Valley wine country. He tells me if his legacy involves what great kids he has, he will be totally happy.

How did we all get so wise? Auker jokes that his weight of 180 pounds is listed in our high school yearbook along with that of other football players. One of the women cracks that she's glad not all of our weights in 1964 are listed. Auker, who looks 20 years younger, still weighs about the same.

I was a beanpole in high school, even my breasts were non-existent. My legs and neck were long. I wore my hair dark and short unlike the fluffy long blonde hair I sport today. I weigh in at 134 now. Carpenter brings a photograph of me in my early *Beacon Journal* fashion writing days posing in stylish hot pants wearing dark hose. Man, was I rail thin.

I'm sure our definitions of happiness and success have shifted through the years. We probably have all felt like a failure at some point and probably all have had feelings of despair. But this group looks like if anyone had lost their way, they've found it now. It's a more mellow experience to be together. That's what is important, certainly not a high school clique membership.

The same could probably be said of how much value we place on our looks. I'm still dedicated to keeping my weight down but when I look in the mirror I know the wrinkle-free face of that high school gal I once was is gone. The lines around my mouth look like a tic tack toe grid. And I wish I would have adhered more closely to my mom's advice to stand up straight. I still slouch terribly.

There are so-so academic public schools such as Ellet where Linda and Tom went and Kenmore where I graced the halls. And then there's illustrious Firestone where Linda's children Scott and Kara ended up.

I remember when Firestone opened in 1963. My senior class is bused to the Fairlawn suburb to take swimming classes at Firestone's new indoor pool. It is embarrassing because we are made to wear these black suits where our nipples are highly visible the minute we hit the considerably chlorinated cold water. We also got a way too much glimpse of the boys' privates as well as they wore Speedo-like swim suits. This was fascinating stuff for my virgin eyes.

Harvey S. Firestone High School is a campus for the International Baccalaureate & Visual and Performing Arts. You can tell a trendy school by the fact it has its own website. Rocker Chrissie Hynde went there along with Olympic diver Phil Boggs, the late astronaut Judith Resnik who was killed in the 1986 Challenger explosion and actress Melina Kanakaredes.

My 'ol *Beacon Journal* pal Pat Snyder says she graduated from the first Firestone H.S. class in 1965. Harvey Firestone Jr. was the commencement speaker and Pat's dad, a lifer at Firestone, was really looking forward to hearing from the rubber potentate. But alas, Firestone was a little disappointing as a speaker, Snyder implies. I wonder if he were having painful flashbacks to when he spoke at Harvey Firestone III's law school graduation in St. Petersburg?

Our high school would have never attracted someone of Firestone's stature as a speaker. You know what though? While we lack glamour, Kenmore gave us what we needed to push off in life. Some of us now are babysitting grandchildren, like me. But two standouts still working are Beverly Bridger, executive director of Camp Sagamore, an Adirondack Great Camp in

Raquette Lake, N.Y., and Frank Saus of Saus Engineering in Annapolis, Md., who has worked in security for the federal government.

At the reunion, I sit at a table with some long-marrieds. I figure with my track record in the marital arena some of the permanence will rub off. Pam Ross, who wed classmate Louis Foster in 1965, went back to school 12 years ago to get a degree and is now a social worker. They've been married for 44 years – and they say youthful unions can't work.

Since most of our lives have played out, everyone has stories I find fascinating to listen to. I wish we could all live at a Sun City-like complex and gather daily for drinks around the pool.

The majority of my classmates – clearly 75 percent – have stayed in the Akron area. They found jobs, raised their families. Yet since 1970, the city has been losing residents from a 275,425 population then to 207,510 today. Not a bad exodus considering the sketchy economy for manufacturing jobs. No longer getting the Rubber Capital of the World billing, Akron is now called a "high tech haven" by *Newsweek* magazine. The city's industry focuses on research, financial and the tech aspects. Goodyear still has its headquarters there but only manufactures racing tires in Akron. And there are small companies such as Gojo, the gooey soap used in public places, located where part of the Goodrich complex used to be.

But there is big news in Akron, according to Firestone spokeswoman Elizabeth Lewis. She works in Nashville, Tenn., because Bridgestone/Firestone moved its headquarters there in 2002, four years after merging with Bridgestone. In Akron, Firestone still manufactures racing tires. But a new 260,000 square feet Technical Center is under construction along Main Street. This will more visibly maintain the company's 110-year presence in town.

This is being built by $68 million from the state, county and city plus federal stimulus dollars for nearby infrastructure repairs.

This stops Akron's Brain Drain, so officials hope. Lewis says this should hold the line for Firestone jobs in Akron. "The 1,000 (jobs) are in existence and will stay in Akron," she says. The structure will be up and running in late 2011.

In 2001, Firestone heir Russell Firestone, a racing fan, told *USA Today* he wished he were born sooner so he could have had a role in managing the company before his family sold it. But could a family-owned tire industry be possible really in today's global economy?

Probably not, says a writer who has covered the tire business for more than two decades. Bruce Meyer, author of "The Once and Future Union, The Rise and Fall of the United Rubber Workers, 1935-1995," says major tire companies are publicly held. "Overseas there might be some Pirelli and Michelin people in the companies still. But there is certainly nothing like what existed with the Goodyear, Goodrich and Firestone families being so visible," says Meyer, who adds, "It's all business today."

It's a new newness for me to see Akron stripped of its strong industrial identity. It's like the windows have been polished to reveal a different world.

And the place is not, I repeat not, a ghost town like some Rust Belt cities. That's a strong comfort like those flannel pajamas I used to wear living here.

Chapter Twenty-Three
The Rich and Poor will Always Be with Us

On my way home from Sunday's high school 1964 bonanza get-together after watching a crushing Cleveland Browns football meltdown (no wonder local malls stock lots of Pittsburgh Steelers merchandise), I spot a sign that rings a bell.

Oh, I couldn't resist pulling into this driveway. It is 2252 E. Waterloo Rd. There's a roadside sign: "Half Day Farm." This is Betty Jaycox's former stomping grounds. My *Beacon Journal* editor lived in a plain tan ranch house on the shores of Springfield Lake. This home still has a "Looker" directional sign in front. This is Jaycox's maiden name. Her father Carl Looker was an early 1920s developer in the Merriman Road area, which, of course, is where the city's emerging rubber barons would live. Springfield is the location of the family's summer home; they lived full-time in the tony West Akron area.

Jaycox loved it here with water lilies and a boat dock at her back door. It is a nice retreat, certainly nothing fancy like all the dinner parties and society events she covered.

This city slicker farm is right down the street from the Goodyear Airdock, former center for blimp research and manufacturing. People probably remember the 1937 Hindenburg disaster (big fiery tragedy in the sky) after which rigid-style airships are abandoned and Goodyear focused on creating blimps. Goodyear now uses blimps for advertising. The airship hangar is still there and remains one of the largest buildings in the world with interior supports. Lockheed Martin now owns this black whale-size Airdock.

So "Half Day Farm" is in an industrial area with the lake used for recreation but not a great location right by the busy road. This is the very first time I've actually seen BJ's compound after reading story after story about the place.

My friend Pat (formerly Ravenscraft) Snyder, the widow of *Plain Dealer* writer Paul Snyder, has a good Betty story. Pat and I worked together at the *Beacon Journal* in the 1970s and she and her then-husband Mark, a politician, were also one of those divorced couples who came from that experience. She says BJ used to make so many lunch dates, she'd forget who she was meeting. So she'd book them all at the Mayflower Hotel's dining room and sit in the lobby at the round upholstered seat and wait to be recognized as the lunch companion du jour arrived.

I do know one thing about "Half Day Farm." In 1981, a favorite *Beacon Journal* photographer Ott Gangl photographed Betty Jaycox in front of her very own picture wall there. It is a collage of all her assignments in photographs through the years, and yes, she's wearing a wig and tight sweater. Gangl photographed me around that time too but I didn't have a photo wall. He took my image to illustrate a first person story I wrote about having rhinoplasty surgery to fix a crooked nose. I'd call this a nose job but my medical insurance paid because my nose was dripping uncontrollable after getting hit by a Frisbee. Gangl's was the best image of me I ever saw – and my new, improved profile was spectacular, I thought.

Once Betty Jaycox, who retired in 1977 and died 10 years later at age 74, faced discrimination in Akron's golf community. She faced the rejection in typical aplomb. It's almost entertaining to read her July 22, 1960 column from the Associated Press Sports Editors online. It seems for the 1960 PGA Championship at Firestone Country Club she wasn't allowed into the press tent because she was a woman.

"Now did you ever hear anything so downright laughable?" asked Jaycox. "I never knew I was so dangerous." She concludes she is making "a big noise" because there she is one woman vs. several hundred men. I would say those guys did not have a chance in hell.

I must e-mail Larry, my ex-husband. "Guess what I did while in Akron. I pulled right into the driveway of 'Half Day Farm,' the former 'estate' of Betty Jaycox. Springfield Lake is pretty but it's nothing special. I felt the ghost of Betty as I looked around."

Larry replies, "Did 'Betty' send a shiver through you? We worked in a newsroom that seems to have had all the clichés that screenwriters put in their versions and Jaycox was certainly one of them."

We old-time newspaper folks are a busybody lot. But then if you're not curious, there is no enterprise.

When I arrive back at my sister's after the reunion wrap-up, I sit with the three newspapers this household has delivered from Canton, Akron and Cleveland.

I read where Tiger Woods is the first athlete to earn $1 billion during his career since 1996, according to *Forbes* magazine. Prize money, appearance fees, endorsement fees, bonuses and his golf course design business give him all the bucks. On a large postcard I picked up at Firestone C.C., Woods is smiling big time holding the gold trophy as the winner of the 2007 World Golf Championships Bridgestone Invitational so Akron has dropped money in that pot.

At the other end of the spectrum, buried on page A2 of the *Beacon Journal* is this one paragraph with a Pittsburgh dateline: "The United Steelworkers Union said Saturday (Oct. 3, 2009) that its members at tire maker Bridgestone Firestone North American Tire LLC ratified new four-year contracts covering 4,500 workers for six plants. The contracts were approved by a two-to-one ratio and will run until July 27, 2013, the union said. The agreement covers plants in Akron; Des Moines, Iowa; Russellville, Ark.; Bloomington, Ill.; and LaVergne and Morrison, Tenn."

And that's the way it is, no reams of newspaper coverage of Akron's labor strife any longer.

I look through Tom and Linda's yearbooks.

In 1960, Tom is lean and good-looking wearing a skinny tie and dark suit for his formal portrait. His hair is a flat top/buzz cut combo. Herbert McLain prefers:

The Caddy, girls, the Fury, drive-ins and dancing. His ambition: To be an architect and design my own home and raise four little architects. And his activities include: Golf, 3,4; basketball, 1,2,3; Sweetheart attendant, 2; softball, 1.

He's not pictured in any of the activity photos but there is a copy of *The Torch* student newspaper dated May 3, 1960. On page three, he's pictured swinging a golf club with this headline: "Golf team wins 3, drops 5 this season." In Ellet vs. Coventry, he golfed 46; vs. Norton, McLain golfed 47, and the Wadsworth match he had a 48. I assume this is his score for nine holes so he is no duffer. His photograph makes him look smallish and tightly wound.

Linda's picture in this 1960 yearbook comes as a surprise. Linda Spring attends seventh grade then and she looks much like her mother with a square face and tightly curled hair. She doesn't know Tom back then and probably didn't even get a "hi" out of him in the hallway. Self-absorbed seniors usually have nothing to do with punk seventh graders.

Linda's formal portrait in 1965 looks more like what I remember she looked like during the PGA job without the teased hair. But she's in absolutely no activity photos and this yearbook doesn't have pages of any information on graduates.

So I have no idea what her ambitions were. I do know she was the "golden child" of her single mother and that will never change.

Tom and Linda met at the Pogo Drive-Inn, a yearbook advertiser. Located at 1324 Canton Rd. (telephone ST4-

6713), it is known for its complete carryout menu, chicken and shrimp, says the ad.

Getting back on the airplane to head back to Florida on Monday, Oct. 5, 2009, two men are reliving the Massillon-St. Ignatius football game in Parma, Ohio. Massillon lost 26 to 21 but it was due to a "late bad call" which one man begins to go over in great detail. He says the Massillon fans were so upset, security had to escort the game's official off the field.

When I return to my island of Tierra Verde, which means green earth, there's news on the radio of a whale being hauled up to the nearby Fort DeSoto county park beach. The 41.5-foot, lactating female Bryde's whale will be buried right down the street from my condo. So goodbye blimps, welcome home to whales buried in the sand.

Chapter Twenty-Four
More Information Not Exactly Pouring In

I'm reminded how foggy our memories become when calling classmates I can find of Tom and Linda's. Like me, they have spent the past 30-plus years dealing with the rest of life going on.

Tom Gentry, who writes musical arrangements and fell in love with barbershop groups at age 16 when he sang in Ellet High school's "The Music Man," isn't much help in recalling classmate Linda.

"I read about her murder in the paper," he says, "way back when. He knifed her, didn't he?" he asks me of how the murder transpired.

The he pauses, and adds, "It was a bad shock."

Gentry says he didn't hang out with Linda back in the 1960s. But he refers me to Kathy Biggs (married name Mishler) who is presently organizing a class reunion for 2010. So I e-mail Mishler.

James Ruddock, a retired truck driver and salesman living in Florida's Orlando area, says, "I could recall the name Linda Spring but I can't put a face on it."

He makes me sound like Pollyanna, liking my high school and college days. He disliked high school ("I hated the place," he hisses) and even gives a big thumbs down to attending classes at Kent State. "I was dumb enough to go back to Kent a few times," he says.

Not that they weren't really good people in school, he adds.

But he was ready to hit the road or in his case serve in the military in the Vietnam War. In Akron, he worked for Consolidated Freightways, a large trucking company. He came to Florida where he was both a mechanic and salesman of heavy-duty trucks.

Victor McLain, Tom's brother, was in Linda's class. He doesn't understand why there's no yearbook photograph or mention of the younger McLain. "I know he graduated," he says.

Ruddock recalls Victor McLain as good-looking, outgoing, popular – all the adjectives one hopes for in high school.

Ruddock steered clear of the Pogo. "I went to drive-ins," he says, "where the muscle cars hung out. Most were in Akron."

He says he wasn't a jock or wasn't chick-a-fied (I guess this means a ladies man).

He says the McLains lived on the south side of Ellet, closer to Springfield. "It's just pretty depressing. It really is to think about murdering that girl," he concludes.

I just picked Charles Spitali's name out of Tom's yearbook because of the unusual surname. I figure he'll be easier to find.

And I do see him listed as a Summit County employee but someone else's name is on the voice mail when I call the number. So I look him up on white pages online.

I get lucky because Spitali lives in Akron and he's home, retiring at age 65 as the night superintendent of a county building.

He says his eyesight is poor and his memory proves to be half-keen about the class of 1960.

"I read about the murder in the paper," he says. "Didn't he stab her about 20 times?" he asks me. I tell him 13, and you can hear his shudder over the phone.

He knew Tom. "He was a little nutsy back in high school but I still never would believe he would do something like that. I don't want to be negative," says Spitali.

When I ask him for details about his "nutsy" evaluation, he says that Tom didn't always act right. I tell him he did have mental problems dating back to his childhood. "I can believe that," replies Spitali.

"I wouldn't say Tom was high strung. I'd say it was more like he didn't care," he says. He says he and Tom double dated a few times. "I can't remember who he went out with. But things would go right by him. He didn't always show the most concern or care for his dates."

He says Tom also was unrealistic about his goals. "If he wanted something, he'd think he could do it no matter what," he says. "He thought he could be a pro golfer. I think that's what he said."

Spitali doesn't go to high school reunions but he had me read what was written about him back then. There is mention of a girlfriend named Phyllis but he didn't marry her. His dog, Daisy, gets a shout out. He liked customized cars. He lists a '51 Merc he owned. He also liked pizza and spaghetti.

He recently sold a '71 Chevelle with his son. "That's the end of that, I think," he ventures, signaling his car selling days are over.

What he remembers before hanging up is that Tom lived with his grandparents. "I think I met his mother Pat once but I'm not sure," he says.

I take a few minutes to scan the printed yearbook interests of Tom's class of 1960. These are pre-Baby Boomers of 245 classmates and their likes are really reflective of the times.

Class of 1960s likes to eat: Pizza, chocolate milkshakes, Brown Derby steaks, Charm candy, pop (soda), shish-ka-bob and then Chinese food – chop suey, chow mein and egg foo young.

One young man states he doesn't want to marry until age 25. What a rebel.

For recreation, classmates like jitterbugging and Beatnik parties. One guy writes he likes cars with souped-up mechanical ability.

One young woman lists her ambition as, "To be Harvey Firestone's private secretary and be happy throughout my life."

With all these 1960s good vibes flowing, Kathryn Biggs (now Kathy Mishler), who's in charge of the class of 1965's reunion in 2010, is scratching her head like everyone else about what went wrong in Linda and Tom's relationship.

Instead of e-mailing me back, she calls. She remembers Linda Spring as one of the quieter ones in school. "I know she must have had some friends. I'll keep trying to figure out who she hung out with," says Mishler.

In the yearbook, Biggs has a tiny, pretty face surrounded by a giant hairdo. I'm looking at that photo as I talk with her just for a comfortable sense of who she is.

She confirms that Victor McLain, Tom' brother, was in her class. "I know there's no picture or not pictured mention of him," she concedes. "I honestly can't tell you if he graduated."

While Linda is quiet in high school, Victor is the opposite, says Mishler. "He was fun loving and out there. When he walked in a room, you knew it."

She recalls the stripper party a few reunions ago when Victor paid for the surprise entertainment at the bowling alley. "It was kinda funny," says Mishler, hesitating.

Did anyone talk about his brother's crime at the reunions through the years? I ask.

"We steered clear of it," she says. "It was so shocking when it happened in our little town of Ellet."

Mishler says the class 45th reunion won't be a "big to-do."

"People are losing interest in attending these," she says sadly. "I'm busy trying to find people," she says, adding she has no idea where Victor McLain is now. I can't find him either although his son, also named Victor, and Scott, Linda's son, are Facebook pals. Victor's last known address is in Colorado.

So I continue with the classmates. Harry Arble sang the "Star Spangled Banner" at an Akron Zip football game in 1962 while a student at the University of Akron. That's the information I spot online about Arble, another classmate of Tom's.

Now Arble is part of the Cornerstone Quartet, a gospel and barbershop group that entertains in nursing homes, he tells me when he returns my phone call.

"I used to buddy around with Tom," says Arble. "Wow, I couldn't believe he killed his girlfriend? Wife?"

"Wife and mother of his three children," I answer.

"I liked him, he was easy going. I was totally shocked when I heard this news through the grapevine."

Arble, who goes by the fun name Harry Canary and wears a yellow vest when playing the guitar and banjo for seniors, says Tom's demeanor in high school must have been misleading.

"He was smiling, happy. Not a care in the world," he says. "But you never know what's on a person's mind."

Arble says his first wife was insanely jealous. "I never dreamed of cheating on her. I couldn't convince her of that but it just became unbearable for me. You never know what pressures a person can take. Of course, I never dreamed of killing her," he says thoughtfully.

I'm thinking back to Tom's fragile condition when he married Linda. A medical report states he has a nervous breakdown when they first marry. But didn't he just serve honorably in the Air Force? That's what his obituary says. I try to get information on his military record but I must go through the maze of the federal government. So I don't know if this will ever lead anywhere.

But I turn to the coroner's report about his death because I think I will need his Social Security number if I am to be successful in obtaining any military report.

I've already mentioned how a Massillon State Hospital physician (Juan Ghersi is his name) states at the time of Tom's death that he had earlier treated Tom for schizophrenia, chronic undifferentiated type.

But what I failed to notice before on the coroner's report is that on Jan. 22, 1980, the probate court released Tom to the custody of Paul Wilkerson, psychologist, for "personal attention and individual psychotherapy."

This must mean Tom is sent to live with his mother while he undergoes this special care. Then on Feb. 10, 1980, he's sent back to Massillon for extended care. The next day, he's sent to Cuyahoga Falls General Hospital with an admitting diagnosis of schizophrenia, paranoid type.

He is discharged from that hospital on March 7, 1980 and "returned home." But not for long. On April 7, 1980, he is returned to Massillon.

Then on May 16, 1980, he's picked up at Massillon by his mother for a weekend visit and that's when he tells her he doesn't want to go back to Massillon. She says, "He appeared despondent." The next day, he dies after ingesting barbiturates.

This shows Tom's back-and-forth of being released into the general population in some detail. He is highly agitated being in Massillon, that's for sure.

I was just reading an article about an investment crook in *Vanity Fair* who says the people he met while in a local jail "yelled and screamed like in an insane asylum."

That's the general public's perception. Was Massillon really so horrible or was it the reminder of his crime – always talking about it in therapy – that Tom hated?

Was Tom deeply remorseful or a villain? I have two early jail photographs of him, line up-like views where he's in prison garb.

He's all but a zombie with dark etched circles around his puffy eyes.

None of the failure he felt justified Linda's murder. But his feelings of despair are evident in these photographs which are passed along to me 20 years ago by then-Akron police chief Phil Barnes.

I compare these to his high school graduation photograph where his face is lit up with a bright smile. And then there's a 1958 Ellet High School yearbook photo I also obtained years ago showing Tom in the back row of the basketball team staring straight at the camera. He is a sophomore and a member of the Junior Varsity. He looks rather blasé.

Chapter Twenty-Five
More Understanding

As a reporter, you pepper people with questions. Then about two minutes after the interview, you think of a handful more questions you should have asked.

I really wanted to talk again with Ken Johns at Heartland, formerly Massillon State Hospital for the Criminally Insane.

I was thinking about those crumbing historic buildings and those crumbling minds inside the new facility. I wanted a little more insight.

My sister and I had joshed about the superintendent's house being open to the public on the grounds of the mental hospital. But that's exactly what is in the works for the gingerbread cottage. Johns says the state and the hospital have spent about $100,000 to fix up the place and are seeking a listing on the Ohio Historical Society Register. New windows, a paint job, fix the roof – all is getting ready for an opening and public tours to view the structure and its antiques.

"We haven't figured out how all this will happen yet," says Johns.

The city of Massillon owns the McKinley building where I saw the theater complex. Johns is sick about its decay. The building is being used to train search and rescue dogs. "It's being destroyed," he says sadly.

The Catholic chapel is run by the Youngstown diocese. Johns says Fr. Matthew Herttna served the chapel for almost 50 years before his death in 2006. I call the diocese. Spokeswoman Nancy Yuhasz says there is a gift shop and weekly mass Wednesdays at 4 p.m. The gift shop is associated with a larger religious goods store in Canton at 4915 Tuscarawas St. W.

"We don't do much with it," Yuhasz says. The diocese has no future plans for the national shrine to St. Dymphna, which is open to the public.

The shrine's website summarizes what this nervous disorders saint hopes to accomplish in the way of healing and understanding. "A surprising large number of patients could leave mental institutions if they could be assured of a sympathetic reception in the world... institutions can help certain cases only to a given extent."

This is more or less the philosophy that Johns has talked about – with the strong qualification that Tom committed a crime. A murder he must pay for, so the justice system rules.

At Heartland, there's also an old warehouse in the back of the 75-acre Heartland property, a former cafeteria, used by the city's parks department for storage. And the cottages where Tom stayed are now part of a 90- to 180-day state-county program for drugs and alcohol recovery.

Which brings up the security question. No patients can't go to church or be free on the grounds without staff trailing along, Johns explains. Heartland serves a spectrum of patients, including those declared innocent by reason of insanity.

If someone like Tom is awaiting sentencing for a violent crime, he'd most likely wouldn't be in this facility where a more homelike atmosphere is fostered today. "Ninety-nine percent would be sent to a forensics hospital like in Columbus," he says, "where there are razor wire fences."

Heartland has indoor security though, such as all units and windows locked, two sets of doors on each wing, security cameras. "Patients aren't considered criminals," he says. "They need treatment and that's our goal. Of course, we are dealing almost always with the non-violent now."

He says, "People come here at their worst. It's our wish for them to get better. Massillon certainly had its own worst moments years ago like insane asylums in general."

And what's on his bedside reading table? "Mad in America," by Robert Whitaker with subtitle, "Bad Science. Bad Medicine. And the Enduring Mistreatment of the Mentally Ill," beginning with the "mad wards" of yesteryear.

Johns emphasizes again that freedom to come and go like Tom experienced is a thing of the past. "You aren't allowed outside without an escort. There are court reviews and doctor evaluations constantly," he reminds.

Johns says the reason there is a nearby tavern, now called Hot Shots, formerly the Elbow Room, is to serve the light industry workers on the same road as Heartland. "Massillon does have a lot of these types of neighborhood bars for a population of 30,000," he says, " I don't know why."

Johns shows he possesses a workplace sense of humor. When discussing the superintendent's cottage, he says that some folks think it's haunted. "After all," he says in a fake eerie voice, "this is an insane asylum."

He presently dislikes the Burger King commercial where they show the "crazy" king being lead away by white coat attendants. "It's an image our industry would rather not put out there," he says. I gave up Whoppers years ago so this commercial doesn't appeal to me from the beginning. But this advertising portrayal of "insanity" is a bit unsettling.

All this talk of benevolent treatment, I wonder if I've been 100 percent fair to J. Edwin Carter, who boosted all those prestigious golf tournaments through the years in Akron. I find Jim Gaquin in Cape Cod who provides some insight. As a writer, it's great to have computer search engines to find people but I wonder what will happen as fewer people have telephone land lines. How will we locate people to interview without White Pages online?

Gaquin, who lives with his wife Lois in West Yarmouth, Mass., was a longtime public relations person for the PGA tours. He's known for his encyclopedia memory of who made what shot and what this meant for the record books.

I reach his wife first and she says he's not home. She remembers Carter vividly and adds they liked his first wife, Mable, a lot. She also recalls living in Dunedin, north of St. Petersburg, as the PGA leased space in the

Dunedin Golf Club in 1945 and stayed there until 1962 when the PGA moved to a large headquarters in Palm Beach Gardens followed by expansion to Port St. Lucie.

Gaquin calls me back the next day and says the same thing about Carter's first wife, Mable, mother of his two children, Julian and Susie. He thinks Mable was a peach although M.J. – my co-boss in Akron – was okay too, he adds.

Carter hired Gaquin in 1956 as a press secretary for the four-man PGA tour staff. "Ed was a visionary. He built the tour up," he says.

"He wasn't a literary guy. He was a wheeler dealer." Carter, a former football player at Northwestern, landed the big time PGA tour director job after doing so well raising money at his home golf course. He lost the permanent director job in 1961 to Gaquin, who was named briefly to run the road show.

This PGA falling out for Carter is because "he made a bad mistake. He had a lot of irons in the fire and the PGA brass thought he was spreading himself too thin."

In those early days of the PGA tour, Carter also ran the Hawaiian Open. "He invited Lois and me to Hawaii but darn we never made it there," laughs Gaquin.

The Gaquins went to Carter's 80th birthday party at his condo in Pinehurst, N.C. Carter had finally slowed down.

But not during his golf career days. Gaquin says one local tournament director thought Carter was a phantom because he'd flash in and out, showing up just enough to do the job – sort of like his sporadic appearances in Akron in 1975. "Ed wasn't a day-to-day guy. He had a Nancy Jupp running his office for years and then he married M.J. and she took over the daily grind," he says.

The 57th PGA book we put together in Akron was a big chunk of change at one time. Before golf on television caught on, says Gaquin, there was a need to raise lots of money for these expensive tournaments. The purse in 1957 was a measly $8,000, says Gaquin, by way of an example of how much golf has grown.

Don Padgett Jr. doesn't remember specifics about Carter other than his pioneer status in marketing. Padgett was the manager at Firestone Country Club from 1980 to 2004. Now he's at Pinehurst, close to the former Raymond Firestone estate where an environmental preserve foundation bought the tire company heir's 417 acres in 2000 for more than $3 million.

Padgett was a club pro in Indianapolis during the 57th PGA. He didn't attend even though his late father (who later became the PGA president) was secretary of the PGA (Don Padgett Sr. died in May 2003). Padgett calls the program books "a thing of the past. If there's an event that isn't an annual such as the PGA or U.S. Open, the books might be handed out as souvenirs to make the sponsors happy. But we stopped doing that with the World Series events at Firestone."

Carter known for those hefty tournament books was a powerful force at one time.

Writer Tim Rosaforte offers a sentimental article on Seminole Golf Club in Juno Beach, Fla., where the golfer Ben Hogan spent 30 days there each year preparing for the Masters.

He writes of Carter: "The (Seminole) tournament (where golfers such as Hogan, Sam Snead, Cary Middlecoff, Arnold Palmer, Byron Nelson) died in the early 1960s because of the falling out between (Christopher) Dunphy (who ran Seminole) and Ed Carter, who in those days ran the PGA Tour. Carter couldn't field an event because all the stars were at Seminole playing the Latham Reed (a two-ball with a club member teaming with a pro)."

Back to Gaquin who believes Carter is a good guy as well as a solid promoter. "He gave me my big break," he adds a few times. Gaquin nicely offers to send me more to read on Carter, a June 1957 *Golf Digest* article.

This arrives promptly in the mail a few days later. The story, titled "Ed Carter, Golf's Man-in-Motion," reinforces what a pioneer Carter becomes after making money for the Baltusrol Golf Club in Springfield, N.J., with his program idea. (I recall the Baltusrol name and look up to see that the New Jersey club is site of the 87th PGA Championship in 2005.) The *Golf Digest* article also calls Carter "moon faced." He was more like half-moon when I met him years later.

But his biggest accomplishment back then is that he gets waived the requirement that PGA championship tournament golfers must have been pros for five years; this opens the doors for golfers such as Arnold Palmer to compete. These fresh stars attract a bigger following and the rest is golf history.

Back when I was winding up my conversation with Gaquin, I mention Linda's death. After expressing his sadness to hear such a thing, he says, "Ed wouldn't have been emotional. I can tell you that," he adds.

Don Padgett III sounds like night and day from Carter. He gets choked up on the phone talking about his late grandfather and you can hear the pride in his voice discussing his father. He calls his staff and the volunteers "great people" and sounds like he means it. Padgett, who was born in 1974, is in his fourth year of being the executive director of the Bridgestone tournament.

He says there are very little phone sales today of the 80,000 plus tickets sold. Instead, databases for e-mails are used. "We don't do a ton of calls because 'do not call' issues arise," he explains.

Padgett remembers himself as a 10 year old playing the "red tees" or forward tees with the legendary Raymond Firestone. "I don't know how old he was then (76, I do the math quickly). But we hit the same distances," he says laughing.

He's proud that the Bridgestone tournament brings close to $1 million for non-profits each year to the Akron area. "So there really isn't much talk about wanting another PGA tournament. That would only come here anyway every 10 to 12 years. Bridgestone is one of only a dozen tournaments in the world where the top golfers play year after year."

When I ask him about women participating on an equal basis, it's almost like he doesn't understand what I'm talking about (ancient history, thank goodness). Yes, women are "allowed" in the press tent and in fact, he says, the *Beacon Journal's* golf writer is Marla Ridenour. The executive committee had a woman as its chairman in 2007.

As for more 1975 comparisons, Padgett emphasizes the heavy program books went the way of the telescope-like, boxy view finders spectators use to carry around. Now fans like light-weight pairing sheets to tote around and sometimes use these for autograph collecting as well.

The 16th hole has indeed been lengthened from Nicklaus' miraculous 625 yards to 667 yards. Padgett calls it "a landing strip." But he says he believes the golfing great would have still made the incredible shot.

Chapter Twenty-Six
Something New About an Old Horror

One night when I'm coming over the Sunshine Skyway bridge from my granddaughter babysitting duties to my home, I see mile after mile of backed up traffic going in the other direction south over the bridge.

The cause is another domestic violence case. The *St. Petersburg Times* provides an in-depth look in a front-page story a few weeks later on October 18, probing for a cause.

A man murders his ex-wife, stuffs her body in a car's trunk, drives to the tall bridge, sets the car on fire and then leaps to his death. Left to sort this mess out is the couple's seven-year-old daughter.

The news story says the woman's family wondered if the killer is mentally ill early in the marriage.

But the explanation for this torment is left dangling. Is mental illness an excuse?, I wonder. Does citing mental illness as a cause act as a salve to help the wounded?

"Children will feel the impact over 30 years later," says Barbara Turpin, policy advocate for the Columbus, Ohio-based Children's Defense Fund.

I have just given her a brief summary of Tom killing Linda and leaving three children as victims as well.

Turpin says the state only expects domestic violence statistics to climb the next few years. "People are under stress because of job loss. Our economic crisis too often means there's more physical violence in the home with the children as witnesses."

According to a report by the child-advocacy organization, Ohio law enforcement agencies received 74,551 domestic violence calls in 2008. At least, 67,000 children were witnesses.

Turpin's idea is to tally the children more carefully. She's not sure what type of form would be used by law enforcement when they are out on a call. But she says this information (age of child, name) could go toward setting up counseling and other services for children.

Of course, she adds, local agencies are terribly pinched with domestic violence programs getting budget cuts in Ohio. Hot lines calls are up 20 percent, she says, for a Columbus agency that helps victims. But the funding is drying up.

"The budgets are getting decimated," says Turpin. There is less and less state money for counties. "Big counties still have counseling and programs but smaller ones are lucky to have shelters."

How are witnesses treated, I ask? I then give her a summary of how Tom is able to see his children for the next five years. "That had to be traumatic," she says. "Children are affected. There's no doubt about that. But again, it's not only an individual case but also what the county can afford."

That's why she's enthused about the statistics and insight she'd like the Ohio Attorney General's office to pick up from law enforcement. These figures of children who witness domestic violence would cost little to gather.

Incident reports are already being filled out. Knowing how many children are trying to cope with the aftermath of violence between their parents could prove vital to communities as they plan their programs and responses.

In an ideal world, Turpin would like programs to head off problems at school. But the statistics would at least provide a starting point of who lives where in violent homes.

How can the same deadly spiral that Linda went through be prevented? This is an important question that unfortunately keeps cropping up. And when violence does erupt, it's sad to hear from the Children's Defense Fund that Ohio ranks near the bottom nationally in support for victims of family violence. Not because helping agencies aren't doing their job. Programs are forced to cut back or turn victims away because of the economy.

And then there's the correlation to the rise in abuse because of lost jobs. I think about what Turpin says but I know that the economy isn't to blame entirely for all this violence; the will to hurt is deep-seated.

Just on a hunch, I next talk with Rex McVicker. I see where he is pictured in Tom's 1960 yearbook next to him alphabetically. So they probably knew each other from classes.

As I look up his phone number, I notice he lives on the same street where Tom's mother and stepdad, Pat and Dominic Sanginiti, resided before their deaths.

McVicker proves to be a powerhouse of information. "Yes, Pat and Dom lived right next door," he says by way of introduction. He says Tom's mother Pat died young of a ruptured neck artery following surgery.

Linda and Tom's tragedy is still fresh in his mind.

On that frosty February morning, he heard on the radio that a man had stabbed his wife 17 times. I try to correct him by saying Tom inflicted 13 stab wounds. But he won't back off. "That's what the radio announced that day," he says.

A Goodyear retiree after 36 years, Rex spends his time as a Red Cross transportation volunteer.

He's sharp and to the point. "I'd see Tom every once in awhile," he says. "I know when he came out of the Air Force he had some problems before being discharged," he informs.

What kind of problems? "Mental problems," McVicker answers. Perhaps the Air Force is too structured for him, I say. "Possibly, that could be it," he answers.

After Linda's murder, McVicker says he stood in his back yard and Tom came over to explain why he killed his wife. "He told me she was fooling around with some man who worked at the PGA office with her," recalls McVicker.

I am flabbergasted. I know the PGA office and there is no one, no how, no way, no time to screw around – period.

"That's impossible," I mutter, barely able to speak. I am physically ill, almost like a punch in the gut after spoiled rotten food. I know Scott had mentioned this but he had also dismissed it readily because he knew his mom's heart. To think Tom is telling people in Ellet that Linda found someone at the PGA office really upsets me.

McVicker pauses. Then he says the neighbors didn't cotton to Tom's being in the community with a manslaughter charge hanging over his head.

"Medication or not, it wasn't comfortable for us to have Tom here," says McVicker.

One time he had to act as peacemaker when an old neighbor named Mr. Clapsaddle took a gun and came across the street to address the problem of Tom living so close after killing his wife. Of course, says McVicker, the old man ended up being carted away for mental observation. (I'm able to verify the Clapsaddle name. Classmates.Com lists a Clapsaddle graduating from Ellet in 1989.)

"It was shocking Tom had so much liberty," he believes. "Then I saw his kids over there after the killing. What must that have been like."

He says he even recalls one time being asked to take one of the McLain children home to the Millers in Fairlawn. "It was a big white house," he remembers.

He adds that during this unwanted drama, he is at a local store and the owner asks casually, "What happened to your buddy?" This unnerved him because he didn't like that people in Ellet are calling him "Tom's buddy."

"Oh my, I thought when he (the store owner) popped that out," says McVicker.

He remembers Linda Spring as quiet and having beautiful eyes. "Tom was the talker in that family."

He knows that Tom is laid off at Firestone but he claims Tom is called back that winter of 1975. "He got into trouble with another worker, some kind of fight, and was fired," he says.

In the yearbook, McVicker writes that he'd like to "some day get hooked into matrimony." He laughs that he didn't exactly get hooked by then student nurse Judy. They married 44 years ago when he was in the Army and have since raised two daughters.

McVicker, next to Tom in the yearbook, has the happy ending.

In December 2009, I receive a letter from the National Personnel Records Center in St. Louis. Tom served in the Air Force on active duty from July 1960 to October 1962. He was inactive from October 1962 to July 1966. He was an airman second class. His not staying in the whole commitment period backs up McVicker's comment about trouble afoot for Tom in the military.

But it remains a horrible shock to hear what McVicker says about Linda being unfaithful. Was Tom trying to be macho? Was he so ill that the most important thing to him was what people thought of him? This cheating crap wasn't concocted by Tom until after he had so much freedom; I saw none of it in his medical file.

Linda's death requires an urgent understanding. My message is a warning: Get away.

And all she kept doing was doodling "Tom & Linda." Linda missed her high school reunions. She missed grandkids. She missed custard cones linked with memories.

Everyone I talk with for years about the Tom and Linda case offers empathy about the losing the job aspect.

Even Peter Bommarito, the late leader of the United Rubber Workers union – he says instinctively, "those bastards," referring to Firestone when a few years later in the late 1970s I'm telling him the murder story as I thought it happened back then.

But a job lay-off has happened to me twice now. My hands are clean of blood.

What didn't happen to me is that I didn't marry a man when I was so young and tender who had major mental problems. I didn't marry someone who treated me like dirt. I was lucky.

Church, friends, family, community – all these would help through bad times. And Akron did have a strong labor union that looked after its own.

I work for the URW part-time after the PGA job ends. I'm walking down the street one day and see J. Curtis Brown, who is URW public relations director. He asks what I'm up too – I knew him as an ex-*Beacon Journal* writer. I say my PGA job is about to end.

So I add the URW to my list of freelance work. Curt is hilarious; his humor is very self-effacing. But he's overburdened with so much traveling for the union.

So I step up and travel some for the union. I don't really know Bommarito for awhile. He's a blur in the office as the 1976 tire labor negotiations are brutal. It's a four month strike that ends with a 35 percent wage increase for workers over three years.

I'm still writing for *Beacon Magazine* plus I do occasional assignments for *Crain's Cleveland Business* and work as a stringer for *Business Week* in Cleveland. This union promotion job which involves speech writing seems odd because I can see both sides. This trait is too ingrained from my reporting. Union and companies are at war, yet isn't the goal to stay in business so everyone has a job? I can't imagine being anti-union or anti-company.

I know this thinking would have been traitorous to say in the URW office. But really, the rank-and-file who run the place are mostly elected union officials such as Bommarito. They have to produce pay raises to stay in office. They, in turn, hire professionals such as lawyers and public relations people to have at their disposal. We never for one moment lose sight for whom we work and what their beliefs are.

But most of us reach a balanced overview. The union pushes hard for all the money it can get for its members and the company plans other ways such as moving plants to non-union states to make profits. Meanwhile, Asia and Europe are coming on as strong competitors.

I couldn't possibly equal Meyer's thorough work on Akron's labor history. His hefty 455-page book, which came out in 2002, shows how the union machine is hugely influential at one time. It's as if union contracts are screaming rock anthems, union leaders rock stars.

I end up working full-time for the union as Curt's assistant for about a year. I travel but my children sometimes get to go along. Once when I took them to Washington, D.C., so we could go to the zoo, Bommarito calls me in my hotel room and says to get downstairs pronto.

I quickly put on a blue, wool, ill-fitting dress. My hair is a flattened mess from the zoo trip. We go by car to Ted Kennedy's house in Virginia where I pose along with Bommarito, Ted and his sister-in-law Ethel.

I'm beginning to have adventures in Akron but unfortunately my marriage to Larry is over. We separate. We divorce. We're thrifty. We use the same lawyer.

I'm laid off from the URW in 1980 when the union hits the skids. All those great benefits but fewer jobs.

I didn't know much details of the politics at the URW like Meyer, managing editor of *Rubber & Plastics News*, chronicles in his book. But I do know that Bommarito would have loved that he received a *New York Times* obituary write-up just like the rubber companies' leaders when they passed. He dies at age 74 in September 1989 after leading the union from 1966 to 1981.

This is the greatest change in Akron for me. In my mind, the bible by Meyer on the United Rubber, Cork, Linoleum & Plastics Workers of America detailing how important the union once is contrasts to the single paragraph on a Firestone labor settlement I read in the *Beacon Journal* when I am in Akron.

I'm thinking if Tom is laid off, then fired from Firestone, the union would have been at his side. But his defense may have taken awhile.

Maybe the PGA could have offered some counseling help to Linda – its staffer – or Firestone could have for Tom.

I guess I'm grasping at rational straws here.

The holidays arrive and so does a greeting card from Genevieve Miller. She signs it simply, "Love, Gen Miller." No woeful note about an ailing spouse. I truly hope she is following her own advice to "Live it up, kiddo."

Fresh air. New energy. Awakening interests – that's what I hope for her.

I love the Bible verse on Genevieve's card from Luke 2:10. "And the angel said, 'Behold, I bring you good news of great joy which shall be for all the people.'"

After reading this, as I hold the festive card in my hand, I realize I've found Linda's memorial in her mother who carries on in faith and love. And in the three bright lights Linda left in this world – her children.

Epilogue

As I am thinking about how to sum up this work with some statistics, another one of those ghastly domestic violence murders is reported in the *St. Petersburg Times*.

"Woman is shot dead; police cite fight over unborn child" reads the March 25, 2010 headline.

A woman is four months pregnant. Her boyfriend reportedly doesn't like that fact. They argue. He shoots and kills her. The mother tells law enforcement she warned her daughter. The boyfriend seemed like the jealous type, she says. He was also disrespectful and didn't treat her daughter well. He didn't want her to have friends. He smashed her cell phone.

I call Brenda Piniella Rouse, who's in charge of communications and volunteers at The Spring in Tampa. Safety. Hope. Renewal. This is the motto for this long-time domestic violence prevention organization.

"Domestic violence is an epidemic," she says, involving all communities, all people regardless of age, economic status, race, religion, nationality or educational background.

One in four women will experience domestic violence during her lifetime.

Intimate partner homicide has been tracked from 1976 to 2005 by the Bureau of Justice. In 1976, 1,307 men were killed by their partner and 1,587 women. In 2005, 329 men and 1,181 women met death at the hands of their loved ones.

In the seventh grade, Linda Spring resembled her mother more – not like she did in later years. (High school yearbook photo)

Linda's grown son Scott McLain is founder of Five Star Fitness Boot Camps. He operates intense exercise programs in Chicago and Columbus, Ohio. He looks so much like his mom and he's friendly like her too. (Courtesy of Five Star Fitness Boot Camps)

Linda Spring, a vibrant redhead, graduated from Ellet High School in 1965. (High school yearbook photo)

Tom McLain graduated from Ellet High School in 1960, a senior when Linda was in seventh grade. (High school yearbook photo)

Tom aspired to be a golf pro but it was his wife Linda who ended up working in professional golf. (High school newspaper photo)

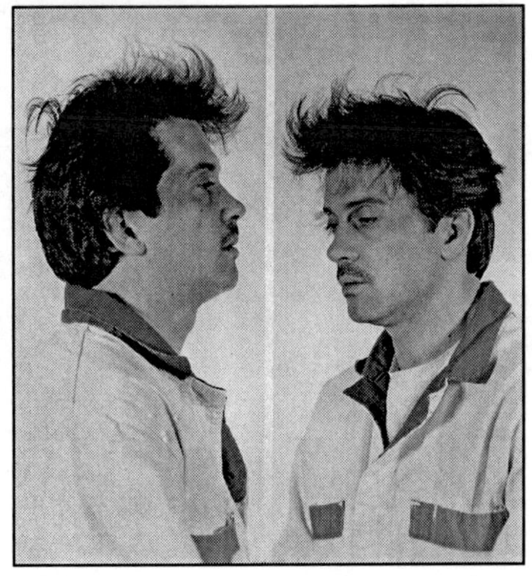

Tom's booking photos after his arrest for Linda's murder. (Courtesy of the Akron Police Department)

My *Akron Beacon Journal* press badge from 1970.

Akron Beacon Journal women's editor Betty Jaycox, pictured at her Half Day Farm home in 1981, strived to keep traditional society news. But young women in the department in the 1970s pushed for more relevant stories such as career and home juggling, abortion and the liberation movement. (Photo courtesy of Ott Gangl)

This is what I looked like in 1981 after my nose surgery. Ott Gangl was the cream of the crop in local newspaper photographers. I still have that candelabra by Akron sculptor Don Drumm in my Florida living room. (Photo courtesy of Ott Gangl)

My 57th PGA Championship badge from 1975.

Harvey Firestone III had a bright future. He graduated from Stetson Law School despite having spastic cerebral palsy. And then he passed the tough law exam. But news of this accomplishment didn't reach him before he allegedly committed suicide in 1960. Here he's pictured with all his 1959 classmates, including Bruce Jacob and Everett Cushman. (With permission of Stetson University College of Law)

This photo was taken right before Diane Elizabeth's birth in 1958. Her father Harvey Firestone III and his wife , Beverly Lou, are at a social gathering. (With permission of Stetson University of Law)

Harvey Firestone Jr. and his wife, Elizabeth, greet Stetson guests at the 1959 graduation ceremony where their son received his law degree. Firestone Jr. gave the commencement speech. (With permission of Stetson University of Law)

Teenage Diane Firestone speaks at the 1974 dedication of the campus swimming pool complex named after her late dad. (With permission of Stetson University of Law)

Larry and I pose with baby Britta and five-year-old son Mark in 1973. I wore that holey Kent State University t-shirt for ages. (Froelich family photo)

I hold a squirmy toddler Britta while Mark tries to look comfortable in a sports jacket in 1974, the same year I went to the 57th PGA Championship job. (Froelich family photo)

My children, Mark and Britta, in 1975. They're so cute no wonder I didn't want a full-time job. But it looks like I could have spent some of that PGA money on haircuts. (Froelich family photo)

Biolography

Akron Beacon Journal, "Who's Who on the Swankiest Street in Town," by Janis Froelich, Sept. 5, 1976, *Beacon Magazine*, Lary Bloom, editor.

Alef, Daniel, *Harvey Firestone: Rubber and Tire Magnate*. Biographical profile.

Associated Press Sports Editors, "Women's Editor Teed Off at PGA." Story posted July 8, 2004; originally published in *Akron Beacon Journal* July 22, 1960.

Cramer, Carol, *People Who Made History* series on Thomas Edison.

Ellet, Mary Jane "Minnie," Akron Women's History, sponsored by the Ohio Humanities Council.

Golf Digest, "Ed Carter, Golf's Man-in-Motion." June 1957.

Highland Square, Akron, Ohio, online newsletters.

Massillon Independent archives.

Meyer, Bruce, *The Once and Future Union, The Rise and Fall of the United Rubber Workers, 1935-1995*. The University of Akron Press.

Nicklaus, Jack with Ken Bowden, *My Story*. Simon & Schuster.

Orr, Lois, "Elzabeth Parke Firestone: Her Couture Collection and Her Role As A Woman of Influence." Master's thesis, August 2006, University of Akron.

Pluto, Terry, *The Curse of Rocky Colavito*. Gray & Company, Publishers.

Seminole Golf Club, "Juno Beach, Florida" by Tim Rosaforte.

Sports Illustrated Vault, "Swinging on A Star" by Dan Jenkins, Aug. 18, 1975. "Developing Crisis in Pro Golf" by Alfred Wright, Dec. 4, 1961.

St. Petersburg Times archives.

SummaCare newsletter, "SummaCare to aid in the preservation of Akron's history. Campus to serve as site to honor the United Rubber Workers." Winter 2003.

Swygert, Michael and W. Gary Vause, *Florida's First Law School, A History of Stetson University College of Law.* Carolina Academic Press.

The New York Times, "Peter Bommarito Is Dead at 74; Led Rubber Workers for 15 Years." Sept. 27, 1989.

The Palm Beach Post, lookback article about press release from the Firestone family regarding Harvey Firestone III's accidental death that he "stood to see the view." Feb. 17, 1981.

Time Magazine, note on Harvey Firestone III's death. May 16, 1960.

Trexler, Phil, "Cleveland Indians: Yesterday & Today." Publications International.

Waterhouse, Helen Stocking, *Akron Women's History,* sponsored by the Ohio Humanities Council.

Acknowledgments

My BCRN (Big Comfort Right Now) is always my husband Ray Bassett. My former husband Larry Froelich provided a wonderful outline for my book. My good friend from my Des Moines, Iowa days, Barbara Ethredge, retired chief counsel for HUD in Birmingham, Ala., provided encouragement early on. Penny Carnathan, an editor at the *Tampa Tribune,* showed me how to write long, oh so long, but tight. Shirley Wittman is always there as a friend. And Pat Snyder, author of "The Dog Ate My Planner," gave me the final push.

Thank you also to: *St. Petersburg Times,* Stetson University of Law, photographer Ott Gangl, Ellet High School, Firestone Country Club, *Akron Beacon Journal,* JimSam Inc. Publishing's Michele Ash and Marcia Freespirit, Tierra Verde Women's Club book club, especially leader Helen Salvini, and Rocky Bluff branch library for continuing to loan me a copy of Jack Nicklaus' autobiography, "My Story."

About the Author

Photo by Ray Bassett

My writing career began when a young managing editor at the *Akron Beacon Journal* took a chance on me. At the time, I was a mother of a one year old, 23 years old, without a driver's license and little self-confidence.

But Robert Giles, now curator at Harvard's Nieman Foundation for Journalists, liked that I had worked toward my career goal so diligently through the years. I was editor of my junior high, high school and finally, at Kent State University newspapers. And I was willing to work in the women's department as it was named in 1969. I wrote engagement and wedding announcements. This work involved coming in on Saturdays so I often think I was doing Giles the favor.

After more than decade of full and part time work at the *Beacon Journal,* where in 1971 the newspaper won a Pulitzer Prize for its May 4 KSU shootings general reporting coverage, I moved to Florida. I had no job but I wanted to be near my parents. The *St. Petersburg Times* hired me but not before editor Andrew Barnes told me, "We don't hire off the street." Again, a young managing editor stepped up and offered me the food writer job. I guess Mike Foley, now an acclaimed professor and associate dean at the University of Florida, figured with my strong Midwest background I would know a spatula from a wire whisk.

I left the *St. Petersburg Times* for the *Des Moines Register* – by this time I was a TV critic – to work for spectacular editor Geneva Overholser, now dean at USC Annenberg's School of Journalism. Then I married photographer Ray Bassett in 1995 and returned to Florida, to the *Times* as a stringer. I began a fulltime job at the *Tampa Tribune* in January 1997 and worked there until July 2008.

Somehow in this journalism career, I squeezed in a job with the 57th PGA Championship, certainly my most memorable of experiences.

Email – janisfroelich@yahoo.com
Website – www.janisfroelich.com

Please visit our website at
www.JimSamInc.com
to order additional copies.

JimSam Inc. Publishing
P.O. Box 265
Lobelville, TN 37097
813.748.9523

LaVergne, TN USA
19 August 2010
193944LV00008B/42/P